The Good Dog Library

Enhanced Dog Care

# Nutrition, Care
# & Grooming
# For the Best in Your Dog

ISBN: 1-879-620-67-7

Belvoir Publications Inc.
Box 2626
75 Holly Hill Lane
Greenwich, CT 06836 USA

Enhanced Dog Care
Nutrition, Care & Grooming for the Best in Your Dog
The editors of *Your Dog* and *Whole Dog Journal*

ISBN: 1-879-620-67-7
1. Dogs-Nutrition      2. Dogs-Care    3. Dogs-Grooming
4. Canine        5. Canine Nutrition            6. Canine Care
Canine-Grooming

Manufactured in the United States of America

The Good Dog Library

# Enhanced Dog Care

# Nutrition, Care & Grooming For the Best in Your Dog

Edited by Diane L. Muhlfeld

Belvoir Publications, Inc.
Greenwich, CT

# Contents

# Preface

Make it a point one day to really observe owners and how they treat their dogs. Chances are, you'll be astonished at the way some people handle their "beloved" pets—tugging and yanking at their collars, yelling at them for their "doggie" (instinctive!) behavior, feeding the cheapest dried and canned food their local supermarket carries; allowing coats to become matted and dirty—even letting them ride loose in the back of cars or pickup trucks.

This is why we emphasize enhanced dog care in this volume, the third in our GOOD DOG LIBRARY series. While anyone can throw any old food at their pets, what sets you apart from the pack is that you've taken the time and trouble to read our books—and that, inherently, means you care more than the average dog owner.

Enhanced care means you'll take the time to find out what's nutritionally best for your dog; you'll make comparisons, read labels—perhaps even concoct a few doggie meals from scratch, once you're convinced these are far better for our four-legged friends than even the so-called "premium" dog foods.

In this volume, we talk about dog fitness, the quality of their environments, how to keep the weight off, whether vitamins should be added to their diets--pretty much how to consider our dogs as individuals, much as we do our own children—each with different needs, to be met in different ways. We'll show you how to de-tox your house (some things are more obvious than others!),the importance of cleaning your pup's teeth, best methods of identification, hot and cold weather care, what car seats and harnesses work best (yes, dogs should be restrained, too)—even how to massage your dog. And we talk about quality time spent with your pet while undertaking necessary grooming chores—best of all, how to make them pleasurable for you both.

After all, if you've gone to the trouble of acquiring a dog—or two, or maybe even more--you might as well take the best care possible of your precious pet. Dogs, like humans, thrive on attention and affection. Enhanced care on your part will help forge a lasting, deep bond between you and man's "best friend."

Diane L. Muhlfeld
Greenwich, Connecticut
September, 2000

# Section I

---

# Nutrition

# 1

# Chow Time:
# A Balanced Diet

*Dog food occupies more shelf space than
baby food in many supermarkets; how do you know
whether you're feeding your dog "the right stuff"?*

Domesticated dogs depend on people to meet their nutritional requirements. As a dog owner who takes this responsibility seriously, you'll want to look closely at two things—your dog's nutritional needs and dog food labels.

## A Balanced Diet

A complete, balanced diet provides your dog with energy and essential nutrients that it cannot manufacture on its own.

■ Protein provides amino acids for tissue growth and repair. Protein should represent about 15 to 25 percent of an adult dog's food intake.

■ Fats are your dog's primary energy source, providing essential fatty acids and transport for fat-soluble vitamins. An adult dog's diet should contain no less than 8 percent fat.

■ Carbohydrates, while not essential, are another important energy source.

■ Vitamins support enzyme function and help regulate nerve-impulse transmission and energy conversion.

■ Minerals support nerve-impulse transmission, muscle metabolism, energy storage and transfer, and blood clotting, among other processes.

■ Water, the "forgotten nutrient," is essential for life. Your dog should always have access to clean, fresh water unless your veterinarian recommends otherwise.

There is a delicate balance in the interactions between nutrients and a dog's cells and tissues. Attentive to that balance, reputable commercial dog-food manufacturers conduct continuous research and development and back the claims on their product labels (such as "nutritionally complete" or "complete and balanced") with actual feeding trials. Veterinarians emphasize the importance of checking to see if a particular manufacturer has noted "feeding trials" on its label to substantiate its nutritional claim

Although a particular food may contain the necessary nutrients, the nutrients are not available to your dog if the food does not taste good and is not digestible. (Ideally, your dog should be able to use 75 percent of the nutrients in its food.) Your dog's system absorbs more nutrients when food is highly digestible (not to mention palatable). Unfortunately, regulations don't require manufacturers to display digestibility percentages on their labels, but you can get that information (and other important statistics) from the manufacturer, many of whom have toll-free nutrition lines.

# Avoiding Excess

According to Dr. Lisa Freeman, clinical instructor at Tufts University School of Veterinary Medicine, "If you feed your dog a reputable brand of dog food that has been proven nutritionally complete through feeding trials, you don't need to supplement its diet with vitamins and minerals unless your veterinarian prescribes them to treat a deficiency or medical condition." In fact, harmful nutrient excesses from overfeeding or supplementing with vitamins and table scraps are far more common than nutrient deficiencies.

# Wet or Dry?

Dog owners face several feeding quandaries. For example, should you feed your dog canned, soft-moist, or dry food? Dry food—the biggest seller—is nutrient dense, less expensive per unit of energy delivered, and convenient. Dry food doesn't spoil quickly, so it's suitable for free-choice (*ad libitum*) feeding. Also, its abrasive action can slow the buildup of tartar and plaque on your dog's teeth. However, some dogs find dry food unpalatable and therefore may not eat enough of it to meet their nutritional requirements.

Canned food has the longest shelf life, but because it spoils quickly once opened, it can't be left out for free-choice feeding. Many dogs, however, find it more palatable and digestible than dry food.

Highly digestible soft-moist food, which often looks like ground hamburger, works well for free-choice feeding. But public concern about preservatives used in processing (and the food's higher relative cost) make it the least-popular commercial dog food.

The least common—and most problematic—feeding option is making your dog's food at home. Although you can concoct homemade dog food that is nutritionally balanced, most veterinarians advise against it. (See subsequent chapters, however.) "People tend to create diets that might be good for them, but are not good for their dogs," observes Dr. Freeman. But if you are truly committed to the idea, design your dog's recipe and monitor its performance with the help of a veterinary nutritionist.

## Popular or Premium?

Another feeding dilemma is whether to buy popular or premium brands. People usually buy premium food from pet stores or pet-supply outlets, while popular (and "store label") brands are available at supermarkets. Many popular brands use variable formulas—that is, the nutrient levels are consistent from batch to batch, but the ingredients vary. Premium brands are usually fixed-formula foods; you get consistent nutrient levels and consistent ingredients. (If you're not sure which formula is used in your dog's food, call the manufacturer.) Keep in mind that many dogs thrive on popular foods that have been proven, through feeding trials, to be nutritionally complete.

Cost may be a consideration, but remember, what really matters is the overall cost of feeding your dog, not how much an individual can or bag of food costs. Premium foods often have higher nutrient density; therefore, compared to less concentrated foods, a smaller amount of a premium brand may meet your dog's needs.

## Reading Between the Lines

*Read past the bold claims that leap out from many dog-food labels and concentrate on the most important information: the statement of nutritional adequacy, the ingredient list, and the guaranteed analysis.*

■ *Nutritional Adequacy Statement: This tells you the food is nutritionally complete for "adult maintenance," "growth," or "all life stages." Most foods claim to meet nutritional levels established by the American Association of Feed Control Officials (AAFCO), but before buying, make sure the manufacturer substantiates its claim with phrases like "feeding studies," "feeding tests," or "feeding trials" somewhere on the label. "A statement that verifies feeding trials were done should be a minimum requirement for the selection of an appropriate diet for your dog," says Dr. Lisa Freeman, clinical instructor at Tufts University School of Veterinary Medicine.*

■ *Ingredient List: By law, ingredients must be listed by weight in decreasing order of predominance. But some companies choose to divide certain main ingredients into constituents to diminish their weight percentage (for example, "corn" becomes "corn gluten" and "flaked corn"). This practice may push ingredients perceived by consumers as "better" to the front of the list.*

■ *Guaranteed Analysis: This list of minimum percentages of protein and fat and maximum percentages of fiber and moisture has a major shortcoming: it doesn't tell you the maximum amounts of protein and fat in the food—information you might need to help manage your dog's obesity, diabetes, kidney disease, or other condition. Note: The guaranteed analysis lists nutrient levels on an as is basis, which won't help you compare one food to another. When comparing canned food (about 75 percent moisture) to dry food (about 10 percent moisture), you must compare dry-matter (that is, moisture removed) nutrient percentages. Your veterinarian or dog-food manufacturer can help you make this comparison.*

# How Much?

The amount of food your dog needs depends on its size (although, per pound, large dogs need fewer calories than small dogs), individual metabolic rate, age, health status, and activity level. A typical dog's nutritional needs change several times over its life span—and even from season to season. (Requirements often decrease during the less-active winter months.)

In general, feed your dog the amount of nutritionally complete, highly digestible food necessary to maintain its optimal body weight and good health. Adjust the amount recommended on the food label according to your dog's response.

Growing puppies, hard-working dogs, dogs living outdoors in cold weather, and lactating bitches have higher per-pound energy and nutrient requirements than the average adult dog. Dogs that sleep all day while their owners work need less fuel than a sled dog or growing puppy. Older dogs tend to be less active than their younger counterparts and therefore require proportionally less energy. (Talk to your veterinarian about your dog's specific nutritional requirements.)

# Rib Test

*Is it time for your dog to lose (or gain) a few pounds? To find out:*

■ *Stand behind your dog.*
■ *Place your hands over the sides of its chest with your fingers spread over the rib cage.*
■ *Slide your hands gently over the ribs.*

*Can you readily feel the ribs? If you can't, your dog is overweight. If the ribs protrude visibly, your dog is too thin.*

# When to Feed

Many of us decide when to feed our dogs based on convenience, but we should also consider other factors. For example, allowing your "chow hound" dog to eat free-choice is an invitation to obesity. And puppies and other dogs with high energy requirements need smaller, more frequent meals to give their digestive systems a chance to absorb the extra nutrients. A veterinarian may also recommend several small daily feedings to help manage the diet of a diabetic dog.

Most dogs will eat whatever you put in front of them (or whatever they can snitch), so arm yourself with knowledge and practice some discipline. Feeding your dog is the most basic form of health care you provide. Carefully read those dog food labels. Call the manufacturer, your veterinarian, or an animal nutritionist if you have any concerns or questions. And monitor your dog's response to its diet by keeping tabs on its weight and general health through regular checkups.

# No Fat Dogs

Obesity is technically defined as body weight 15 to 20 percent over a dog's optimal weight. And overfeeding is the most common cause. (But before you assume that your feeding style is responsible, ask your veterinarian to check for potential medical causes.)

Portly pups are at increased risk of developing diabetes mellitus and skin ailments. Obesity also exacerbates certain orthopedic, heart, and nervous-system diseases. Fat dogs are also higher-risk surgical patients, and they tend to have lower resistance to infection.

Although overfeeding dogs at any age can cause obesity, overfeeding during puppyhood can predispose a dog to lifelong obesity. While puppies are growing, both the number and size of their fat cells increase. Reducing the number of fat cells is much more difficult than shrinking their size.

Studies show that the incidence of obesity increases with age, and is more common in neutered dogs. It is an easier condition to prevent than treat. Treatment is straightforward but challenging—you have to make sure your dog's caloric intake is less than its energy expenditure. To slim down, an animal must take in less energy than it expends. Given this fact, veterinary treatment for obesity usually focuses on controlled reduction of calorie intake and increased exercise compatible with an individual dog's health. To help your dog successfully lose weight, collaborate with your veterinarian, because frequently owners need to change their behavior.

Veterinarians also frequently recommend a high-fiber diet for overweight dogs. (Fiber provides few calories but plenty of bulk, giving Fido a "full" feeling.) Many veterinarians suggest breaking up the dieter's daily food allotment into several feedings so "Big Brown Eyes" is less likely to beg for sinful snacks.

If your dog's overall health permits, moderate exercise—such as brisk daily walks—is the best way to expend energy. "Most dogs out in the yard by themselves don't get much exercise," observes Dr. David Dzanis, a veterinary nutritionist at the Food and Drug Administration's Center for Veterinary Medicine, so owners have to make a point of scheduling in daily exercise for their dogs. (Researchers also believe regular exercise may increase a dog's at-rest metabolic rate, boosting energy consumption even when Fido is napping.)

Give your dog the low-calorie diet—nothing else—during the weight-loss campaign. All family members must "buy in." And don't forget—attention is a healthy substitute for food treats

# Pharmacological Aids

Any dietary and exercise regimen involves a substantial commitment of time, effort, and willpower on the owner's part. Hence, over-the-counter "diet pills" that claim to boost the effectiveness of traditional weight-reduction programs are appearing on the market. While these products may attract owners who find it difficult to stick to prescribed regimens, there is no proven "quick fix" for obesity. (Always check with your veterinarian before giving any dietary supplement to your dog.)

One new diet-aid product (marketed as Fit 'N Frisky™) contains chromium nicotinate and hydroxycitric acid (HCA). The manufacturer claims that these components impede the conversion of calories to fat. Chromium nicotinate theoretically boosts the efficiency of insulin (the hormone that helps cells consume glucose—the body's main energy source). And HCA appears to disrupt the chemical process that converts excess carbohydrates into fat, helping the body instead convert carbohydrates into glycogen (the storable form of glucose). In turn, the brain reads high glycogen levels as a signal of satiety and responds by sending appetite-suppressing messages to the body. However, dogs are physiologically capable of storing only so much glycogen, and no one knows how (or if) HCA affects the energy-conversion process once a dog reaches its glycogen-storage capacity.

Despite the largely theoretical nature of the claims made for HCA and chromium nicotinate, at least one unpublished study suggests that supplementing a dog's diet with both these compounds may help achieve greater overall weight loss. But a computerized analysis of the study data showed that weight-loss differences between the two groups that received the supplements and the two groups that did not were statistically weak. Clearly, further studies are necessary to confirm the beneficial effects of chromium nicotinate and HCA on dieting dogs.

Owners contemplating the use of diet-aid products should also know about the possibility of harmful side effects. The Food and Drug Administration has tested neither chromium nicotinate nor HCA for safety and efficacy in dogs. But preliminary cell studies suggest that chromium compounds may increase the risk of chromosome damage, and independent investigators have linked HCA to liver enlargement in chickens.

Before jumping on the diet-pill bandwagon, step back and consider two things. First, these products are not substitutes for carefully tailored adjustments to diet and exercise. And second, there is (alas!) no effortless way to lose weight. ❖

# 2

# Feeding Fido:
# Debunking the Myths

*Caring owners match what they feed their dog
to its life stage, breed, activity level,
size and overall health.*

Over the course of a lifetime, dogs change—and so do their nutritional needs. Their food intake must be balanced against where they are in their life cycle, along with numerous other factors. Frequently, however desirous of giving their dogs "the best," some owners make erroneous—and potentially harmful—dietary assumptions.

## Myth: More Is Better

If an adult-maintenance diet with 20 percent protein is good, then 35 percent protein must be better. Right? Not necessarily. While excess protein does no apparent harm to healthy dogs, too much protein may harm dogs with poorly functioning kidneys.

Healthy adult dogs require a minimum of 18 percent protein and 8 percent fat (on a "water removed" dry-matter basis) to maintain good health when at rest and free of stress. But hard-working dogs, canine athletes, or dogs that stay outdoors in cold weather may need greater quantities of certain nutrients—especially fat, which provides energy.

But when a dog's intake of calories (found most abundantly in fat, carbohydrates, and protein) consistently exceeds the calories it expends, the dog becomes obese.

Beginning in 1998, new state regulations, based on recommendations from the Association of American Feed Control Officials, will require that label claims of "lite" (lower in calories) and "lean" (lower in fat) adhere to strict nutritional guidelines.

# Myth: Pups Should Be Plump

Growing puppies do require more calories per unit of body weight and different concentrations of certain nutrients than adult dogs. You should therefore use puppy food with higher levels of protein and fat than in adult-maintenance food.

But don't go overboard. If puppies ingest too much energy-dense food, they may be headed for lifelong obesity. Both the size and number of fat cells increase in growing pups. Obesity caused by too many fat cells is difficult to combat because reducing the number of fat cells is much harder than reducing their size.

Moreover, too-rapid growth predisposes large-breed puppies (more than 65 pounds when mature) and giant-breed puppies (more than 90 pounds when mature) to skeletal problems such as hip dysplasia and osteochondrosis (both of which lead to arthritis).

Because high-potency puppy foods promote growth, experts suggest that owners of large- and giant-breed pups either feed less than the recommended amounts or use newly available growth formulas developed especially for large and giant breeds.

The new formulas promote slower, more gradual skeletal and muscular development because they are less calorie-dense and contain lower levels of calcium and phosphorus than traditional puppy foods.

# Myth: Old Dogs Need "Senior" Diets

Some people think every dog over 7 years of age needs a low-fat, low-protein "senior" diet rather than regular adult-maintenance food. But "older dogs are not a homogeneous group," cautions Dr. Lisa Freeman, assistant professor at Tufts University School of Veterinary Medicine. "Treat your older dog as an individual and tailor its diet to its health, body condition, and activity level."

Veterinarians once also encouraged owners to feed older dogs low-protein victuals to reduce the risk of kidney disease. But recent studies show that restricting protein below the adult-maintenance level is unnecessary for most healthy older dogs.

While slower metabolism and decreased activity can lead to weight gain in older dogs, some elder "statesdogs" have a propensity to lose weight. To accommodate the varying needs of senior dogs, one dog-food manufacturer sells a senior diet for overweight elders and another formula for "skinnies."

Remember, your dog is "one of a kind" and will not automatically require a special diet because it's young, old, or in between. Discuss diet with your veterinarian or a veterinary nutritionist. And when reading dog-food labels, be careful to distinguish between genuine nutritional information and marketing hype. ❧

# 3

# Feeding Newborn Puppies

*If you're the surrogate Mom it can be an
around-the-clock job for several weeks.
But look at the rewards.*

In an ideal world, all puppies would receive nurturing and sustenance from their moms (dams) during the first few critical weeks of life. Alas, some dams contract diseases and can't nurse, some reject their puppies, and some newborns lack the physical strength to nurse. In such unfortunate cases, humans can help. But if you accept the role of surrogate dog mom, be prepared to stay busy around the clock for several weeks. There may also be heartbreak involved; some pups don't make it despite their human surrogate's conscientious efforts.

Early-puppyhood caretakers have two main jobs: providing a warm, draft-free environment (young pups can't regulate their body temperature and are vulnerable to chills) and feeding the pup the correct amount of appropriate nourishment at the right time.

## Nothing Like Mom's Milk

In addition to essential nutrients, a dam's first milk (colostrum) contains antibodies that provide newborn pups with temporary immunity against disease. If at all possible, puppies should ingest colostrum during the first few hours after birth. If mom or another nursing "foster dog" is not available, you'll have to hand-feed the puppy—and do your best to isolate it from sources of infection to compensate for the lack of maternally provided immunity.

To make sure hand-fed pups receive proper nutrition, most veterinarians recommend commercial milk-replacement formulas, available as ready-to-feed liquids or mixable powders. "Homemade formulas are less convenient, and not all recipes provide adequate nutrition for a newborn puppy," notes Dr. Lisa Freeman, assistant professor and nutritionist at Tufts University School of Veterinary Medicine. Cow's milk alone is definitely inadequate because it lacks sufficient calories, protein, calcium, and phosphorus. Whether you use a commercial or homemade formula, keep it refrigerated to prevent growth of harmful bacteria and warm each serving to about 100 degrees Fahrenheit just before feeding time.

# Tube or Bottle?

You can get formula into a pup through either a nipple bottle or feeding tube. Bottle feeding takes longer and increases the risk that the puppy will accidentally inhale formula into its lungs. Tube feeding, which involves delivering formula through a feeding catheter passed into the puppy's stomach, is generally safer and faster—and the most practical method for a newborn that lacks a sucking reflex. Both techniques require some expertise, so ask your veterinarian or an experienced puppy raiser for a demonstration. With either method, it's important to wash all feeding utensils in hot, soapy water after each use.

# Weight Watching

When using commercial preparations, follow the mixing instructions and weight-based feeding guidelines on the label, remembering that you may need to increase or decrease listed amounts to suit individual pups. "For the first couple of days, it's better to err on the side of underfeeding," says Dr. Freeman, who explains that overfeeding (or feeding a formula that's too concentrated) can result in diarrhea. Young pups dehydrate rapidly, so if diarrhea persists for more than 24 hours, have your veterinarian check out the pup. During a pup's first week, it should be fed every 2 hours. Subsequently, feed the total daily amount over six equally sized and spaced-apart feedings.

Steady weight gain is the best measure of whether a hand-fed pup is receiving appropriate nourishment. In general, a pup should gain 1 to 2 grams of weight daily for each pound of its expected adult weight. For example, a dog you anticipate will weigh 50 pounds as an adult should gain 50 grams (1.75 ounces) to 100 grams (3.5 ounces) per day. Keep accurate records of how much formula the pup consumes at each feeding and how much weight it gains each day.

# The Tail End

Until a dog is about 3 weeks old, it can't urinate or defecate on its own. To stimulate these important bodily functions, gently massage your pup's anal and genital area after feeding with a cottonball dipped in warm water.

If you embark on the demanding task of hand-rearing a puppy, it could be the most rewarding canine caretaking experience you ever have. But first, honestly ask yourself if you have enough time and energy. If not, your veterinarian or local humane society may be able to find a suitable surrogate. ❧

# 4

# Premium Foods:
# Are They Worth It?

*Should you spring for the more expensive "premium" labels or feed Fido the "popular" supermarket brands.*

For many of us, providing a raw food diet is inconvenient, time-consuming and expensive. So, for those who have gotten used to the ease of feeding dried dog food out of a bag, we can help you become an informed consumer in the "popular" vs. "premium" foods debate.

Cup for cup, premium foods typically contain more calories and are more digestible than popular brands, so it takes less premium food to meet your dog's needs. Also, smaller amounts of highly digestible food mean smaller stools—another advantage of premium food.

Another difference between popular and premium brands is the batch-to-batch consistency of ingredients in the food. Most popular brands use variable formulas; this means the nutrient content listed on the label's "guaranteed analysis" is uniform from batch to batch, but the actual ingredients may vary depending on cost and availability. Premium brands are usually fixed-formula foods, delivering consistent nutrient levels with the same ingredients from batch to batch.

"Premium" dog foods include those foods that are priced at $1 dollar per pound and up, and supposedly contain ingredients that surpass in quality the lower-priced brands. Our analysis found that there are big differences in the premium category. High prices don't necessarily mean high nutritional value. And some so-called "premium" vendors still use artificial preservatives and coloring. Still, we found some very good buys at acceptable prices!

# Why Quality Is Important

Not all dried foods are created equal. Experts in canine nutrition, like experts in human nutrition, differ in opinion about what is best, and accordingly, there are dog foods of every conceivable combination on the market.

How do you choose? Informed decisions rest on several factors, including the food content's type, quality, and digestibility. Cost, too, plays a role. Dog foods with good quality ingredients are simply more expensive than foods containing only by-products.

How can you determine whether the ingredients are of the best quality? Admittedly, it's hard, since the regulations that dictate what food products may and may not go into dog food have largely been determined by the pet food makers. Unfortunately, practically no food item or by-product is too disgusting, diseased, or rotten to be passed over for the manufacture of dog food. Condemned parts and animals that are rejected for human foods are often re-routed to pet food manufacturers.

In fact, there is a phrase, "4D," for the types of meat that make their way from human food manufacturers to the pet food makers. It means, any meat that is dead, dying, diseased, or disabled. Even animals that have died and have begun to decompose are used. "Meat and bone meal" sounds innocuous, but it is primarily composed of meat that is too far gone to be considered for inclusion into pet foods that call for "meat." Instead, it is sterilized and rendered, to be born anew as "meat and bone meal," a major component of many pet foods.

What kind of nutrients, if any, can possibly survive such a journey? Not many, but don't worry, manufacturers will add protein from cheaper sources, like corn gluten, soybean meal, and rice gluten, and then "fortify" it with vitamins and minerals, preserve it with artificial preservatives, make it better looking to the owner with artificial colors, and spray on a last-minute coating of vegetable oil to encourage dogs to eat it.

Fresh, wholesome meat and whole grains contain all the nutrients that dogs need, but it's very hard to find dog foods that contain those things and nothing else. Pet food makers argue that it's very hard to make a pet food with just those things and get pet owners to pay for it; the price would be too exorbitant. Some have started to move toward less-chemical laden foods with higher quality ingredients, but the shift in consciousness required is so huge, that these efforts are regarded by many holistic veterinary practitioners as next to useless.

# You've Got To Start Somewhere

While some admirable souls in the trenches of holistic medicine insist that only raw meat will do, we recognize that many readers want to feed dried foods—and that some guidance may be helpful.

At a minimum, we recommend that you reject any dog food containing any of the following, each of which has been implicated in canine health disorders:

■ Artificial color.

■ Artificial preservatives like BHA, BHT, potassium sorbate, sodium nitrate (used for dual purposes, preservative and coloring), and especially, ethoxyquin.

■ Sugars and sweeteners like corn syrup, sucrose, and ammoniated glycyrrhizin (added to attract dogs to otherwise unappealing fare).

■ Anything with the term "flavor" in the ingredients list (like sugar, this indicates the contents doesn't have enough of its own good flavor – not the hallmark of quality ingredients).

■ Propylene glycol, which is used to keep certain foods moist.

■ Foods with corn (one of the least expensive grains available to food makers) and/or corn by-products listed more than once in the first five ingredients.

Consider, too, the types of meat in the food. If a food has one or more questionable source of protein it should be rejected. Foods that have whole meat (listed simply as lamb, chicken, beef, etc.) in the top three ingredients are recommended.

Look for whole foods like rice, wheat, and eggs, and foods that are kept fresh with natural preservatives like vitamin C and E (often listed as mixed-tocopherols).

Also, look for something called AAFCO approval; it's not a very tough standard, but it's the only one for dog food there is.

And – we can dream on, because we have yet to see a food that offers it – if you were ever to find a dog food that offered certified organic meats, grains, and vegetables, we'd suggest you buy a lifetime supply and put it in a refrigerated vault.

# Test Your Knowledge

Below, you'll find a list of 13 dogs foods commonly known to the average dog owner. With the exception of Kibbles 'N Bits, they are considered "premium" foods by the pet superstores (and priced accordingly), and a few are what must be considered "superpremium," formulated and marketed toward those looking for the very best. Kibbles 'N Bits represents the high end of low-cost foods, and we've included it for comparison purposes.

We suggest you look over the ingredients (we've listed the first 10 ingredients only) and nutrition information. Then, though you'll probably be able to take on this task when you're done comparing) we'll tell you which ones we like, which ones we don't, and why.

You'll notice four basic values are also presented for each food: the minimum percentage of crude protein and crude fat, and the maximum percentage of crude fiber and moisture. Federal law requires that these values are printed on all dog food labels.

The percentage of protein in a food must always be viewed in context with the actual protein sources in the food. It's possible for the manufacturers to "load" a food with crude proteins that are virtually indigestible, and thus, useless to the dog. If the protein level of a certain food is higher than average, look for its source in the list of ingredients. Rich in essential amino acids, meats are considered the best source of protein.

The amount of protein and fat a food has should be roughly proportional, since there are metabolic interactions between the two.

*How do you choose? You can't even begin until you've read the tiny print of the ingredients list, and learned the difference between, say, "beef" and "meat and bone meal."*

The more protein a food has, the more fat it should have. The amount of crude fiber and moisture in each dog food is expressed on the product labels as a maximum percentage. Crude fiber is basically the indigestible matter in the food. Moisture is the amount of water in the food; all foods need a certain amount of moisture to be palatable.

We've arranged our sampling according to their price per pound, since the cost of the food affects and informs most dog owners more than any other factor. Each brand of food is packaged in a variety of sizes; we've selected similar weights to compare prices. Just as when buying human food in bulk, these dog foods are less expensive if bought in larger amounts.

Where possible, we sampled the same type of food, choosing each company's lamb-based product, so you could compare differing but equivalent formulations. Again, before you make buying decisions, review the terms defined on the next page. Your opinion of some foods may change when you learn the meaning of some common phrases on dog food labels. For instance, why is the word "Formula" in so many dog food titles? As you'll find, it means that the ingredient or combination of ingredients named in the title constitute anywhere from 25 percent to 94 percent of the contents. Unfortunately, there's no way to know whether the total is closer to 25 or 94 percent.

# What's in the Bag?

Below are the AAFCO definitions of the most commonly used phrases that describe the ingredients in dog food:

■ **Meat**: (e.g., lamb, beef, chicken) – "Meat is the clean flesh derived from slaughtered mammals and is limited to that part of the striate muscle which is skeletal or that which is found in the tongue, in the diaphragm, in the heart, or in the esophagus; with or without that accompanying and overlying fat and the portions of the skin, sinew, nerve, and blood vessels..."

■ **Poultry**: "Poultry is the clean combination of flesh and skin with or without accompanying bone..."

■ **Meat Meal**: (e.g., lamb meal, beef meal) – "Meat Meal is the rendered product from mammal tissues, exclusive of any added blood, hair, hoof, horn, hide trimmings, manure, stomach and rumen contents except in such amounts as may occur unavoidably in good processing practices...."

■ **Poultry Meal**: "Poultry Meal is the dry rendered products derived from a combination of clean flesh and skin with or without accompanying bone..."

■ **Meat and Bone Meal**: is the rendered product from mammal tissues, including bone, exclusive of any added blood, hair, hoof, horn, hide trimmings, manure, stomach and rumen contents, except in such amounts as may occur unavoidably in good processing practices..."

■ **Meat By-products**: is the non-rendered, clean parts, other than meat, derived from slaughtered mammals. It includes, but is not limited to, lungs, spleen, kidneys, brain, livers, blood, bone, partially defatted low temperature fatty tissue, and stomachs and intestines..."

■ **Poultry By-products**: must consist of non-rendered clean parts of carcasses of slaughtered poultry such as heads, feet, viscera..."

■ **Poultry By-Product Meal**: consists of the ground, rendered, clean parts of the carcass of slaughtered poultry, such as necks, feet, undeveloped eggs, and intestines, exclusive of feathers, except in such amounts as may occur unavoidably in good processing practices..."

■ **Animal By-product Meal**: is the rendered product from mammal tissues, exclusive of any added hair, hoof, horn, hide trimmings, manure, stomach and rumen contents...This ingredient definition is intended to cover those individual rendered animal tissue products that cannot meet the criteria as set forth elsewhere in this section..."

If a product label says it is "**Beef Dog Food**," it must be at least 95 percent beef, minus the water required for processing. If a label identifies the product as a beef **Dinner**, **Platter**, **Entree**, or **Formula**, beef must comprise anywhere from 25 to 94 percent of the ingredients. If the dinner is a **Combination of Meats** (i.e. "lamb and rice dinner"), the lamb and rice combined must comprise at least 25 percent of the content.

A food called "**Brand X with Chicken**" must contain at least three percent chicken. If the label says the food has a "**Lamb Flavor**," it has to have a "detectable flavor," although who gets to detect it, we're not sure.

# More Labeling Tricks

The ingredient responsible for the greatest amount of weight in the bag is listed first. "Water sufficient for processing" sounds reasonable, but if it comes first on the label of a canned food, you're paying for water more than anything else.

Sometimes the manufacturers "split" a lesser-quality food into two components, in order to list them in smaller quantities than another, higher-quality food. For example, if a label reads, "Beef, ground yellow corn, rice, corn gluten meal," it appears that there is more beef than anything else in the sack, but the total weight of the corn (ground yellow corn plus corn gluten meal) may outweigh the beef. And because the labels don't require the relative percentages of each ingredient to be listed (neither do human food labels), it's hard to know by what margin the corn outweighs the beef.

# Who's In Charge Here?

*In the U.S., the Food and Drug Administration oversees basic aspects of the production of pet foods. The FDA's "Code of Federal Regulations" requires that pet foods be pure and wholesome, contain no harmful or deleterious substances, and be truthfully labeled. In addition, some states impose and ostensibly enforce their own labeling regulations.*

*If you look at the bag containing your dog's favorite food, however, you'll likely see text noting approval by the Association of American Feed Control Officials (AAFCO), a non-government advisory body with representatives from all states. Most dog and cat food manufacturers voluntarily comply (they don't have to) with a set of standards set by the group. These standards include protocols for ingredient and product names, flavor designations, and nutritional adequacy statements.*

*There are two types of approvals to be gained from AAFCO. The more stringent (used loosely here) requires a feeding test of the prospective dog food. If the food passes the test, the dog food manufacturer gains the right to say, "Animal feeding tests using AAFCO procedures substantiate that (insert name) dog food provides complete and balanced nutrition for all life stages."*

*What's the test?*
■ *Eight dogs older than one year must start the test.*
■ *At the start of the test all dogs must be of normal weight and healthy.*
■ *A blood test is to be taken from each dog at the start and end of the test. The blood test measures the four*

*blood values they deem most important. In comparison, a standard diagnostic profile of blood taken in your veterinarian's office measures some 25 blood values.*
■ *For six months, the test dogs must eat only the test food.*
■ *The dogs finishing the test must not lose more than 15 percent of their body weight.*
■ *During the test, none of the test dogs are to die or be removed due to nutritional deficiencies.*
■ *Six of the eight test dogs must finish the test.*

*While the AAFCO feeding trials don't constitute a very stringent test (six months is barely long enough for the test dogs to display certain deficiencies), keep in mind that they are the most rigorous test the food will receive from any agency. If a manufacturer wishes to forego this trial, they can still gain the second type of approval from AAFCO, in which an analysis of the food shows that it meets the nutrient requirements of dogs. However, there are no criteria to determine whether those nutrients are in a form that the dog's body can assimilate.*

*While both reviews fall short of providing a serious test of the foods' ability to keep a dog in peak health throughout his entire lifetime, they guarantee, at least, the food does contain nutrients. If a food label fails to include one of the two approvals, one would certainly wonder whether anything was in the bag at all.*

# We Recommend

■ **California Natural**: This food is our clear-cut winner, based on small and simple list of top quality ingredients. In fact, its advertising boasts the irrefutable fact that California Natural has the shortest list of ingredients in the industry. This food contains no artificial preservatives, colors, or flavors, and is affordable to boot. It can be found in selected health food stores and independent pet stores.
■ **Flint River**: Another top-quality (human-grade) food with less than the top price. At risk of limiting their sales, the maker of this food does not make it available to pet store shoppers. Instead, it must be ordered directly from a company representative and is shipped directly to you from the factory, ensuring the ultimate in freshness.

■ **Petguard Lifespan**: It doesn't take a brain surgeon to pick the most expensive food or the one with the highest protein levels as a candidate for quality ingredients. The maker claims the chicken used is human-quality and free of growth hormones. So far, so good. But why so much corn?

# Not Recommended

■ **Kibbles "N Bits**: It's not fair to compare this with the rest; it's not considered a premium food. But after the product was called a "winner" in *Consumer Reports* 2/98 issue for being the unanimous favorite of their panel of test dogs, we had to comment. Kibbles 'N Bits is the canine equivalent of Twinkies. The ingredients are led off with corn, and each of the animal-protein ingredients are very low quality: beef and bone meal, animal fat, animal digest. Water and corn syrup also appear in the top 10 ingredients, explaining the high moisture content; propylene glycol keeps it sealed in.

■ **Breeder's Choice Avo-Derm**: A much healthier concoction, but we're not crazy about two things. First, this was the only dried dog food we could find that opted not to pursue feeding trials approved by AAFCO. Instead, its manufacturer sought the lesser AAFCO approval and had its nutrient requirements verified in the lab only. That, and its scarcity of animal proteins (it does contain fish meal, fairly low on its contents list), make us wonder about its palatability. This lack of meat could be used as a tool to market this food to owners of dogs with meat allergies, but interestingly, its packaging makes no note of this absence. No artificial colors, flavors, or preservatives.

■ **Waltham Lamb Meal & Rice**: Despite its high price, often indicating quality ingredients, this food features a nutritionally empty vegetable filler (beet pulp), two questionable meat sources (lamb digest and animal fat), and salt (another taste-tempting ingredient) in the top 10. Topped off with not one but three artificial preservatives – on behalf of our dogs, we'll decline.

# How Much Should You Feed Fido?

*Consider the following factors:*

■ ***Breed size**: Small breed dogs weighing less than 20 pounds need about 30% more calories, pound for pound, than dogs in the 20 to 75 pound range. Large breed dogs*

## PREMIUM FOOD INGREDIENTS

| Dog Food | Price/ Lb. | % Crude Protein | % Crude Fat | % Crude Fiber | Moisture |
|---|---|---|---|---|---|
| *Kibbles 'n Bits Chicken & Beef Flavor | $0.97 | 19 | 8 | 4 | 18 |
| California Natural | $1.08 | 21 | 11 | 4.5 | 10 |
| Pro Plan Beef & Rice Formula | $1.19 | 25 | 15 | 3 | 12 |
| Nutro Max Maximum Nutrition | $1.20 | 26 | 16 | 4 | 10 |
| Iams Lamb Meal & Rice Adult Formula | $1.25 | 22 | 12 | 5 | 10 |
| Innopet Veterinarian Formula | $1.36 | 20 | 12 | 4 | 11 |
| **Breeder's Choice Avo-derm** | $1.39 | 20 | 8 | 4 | 10 |
| Nature's Recipe Vegetarian Formula | $1.50 | 18 | 8 | 4.4 | 10 |
| Science Diet Lamb Meal & Rice Formula | $1.60 | 19.5 | 13 | 2.5 | 10 |
| Flint River Chicken Meal & Rice Formula | $1.62 | 23 | 12 | 4 | 10 |
| Waltham Lamb Meal & Rice Formula | $1.87 | 21 | 8 | 5 | 12 |
| Eukanuba Lamb & Rice Formula | $1.90 | 23 | 14 | 4 | 10 |
| PetGuard LifeSpan | $2.12 | 26 | 15 | 4 | 12 |

*This is not a premium food according to our price criteria. We've listed it here to illustrate how even foods we don't recommend can still be considered "nutritionally complete and balanced" by the AAFCO. Compare its ingredients to those of our favorites, noted in the text.*

**First 10 Ingredients**

Corn, soybean meal, beef and bonemeal, wheat flour, animal fat, water, wheat middlings, corn syrup, animal digest (source of chicken and beef flavors), propylene glycol.

Lamb meal, ground brown rice, ground rice, sunflower oil, vitamins/minerals. Natural preservatives, no artificial colors or flavors.

Beef, brewer's rice, ground wheat, ""corn gluten meal, beef tallow, chicken meal, dried beet pulp (5%, source of fiber), egg product, deflourinated phosphate, dried whey.

Chicken meal, wheat flour, ground whole wheat, rice bran, poultry fat, corn gluten meal, ground rice, lamb meal, yeast culture, calcium carbonate.

Lamb meal, rice flour, ground corn, ground grain sorghum, fish meal, rice bran, animal fat, dried beet pulp, dried egg product, chicken digest. Natural preservatives.

Lamb meal, rice, barley, corn gluten meal, oats, lecithin, chelated minerals. Natural preservatives, no artificial colors or flavors.

Wheat flour, meat meal, ground rice, wheat middlings, dried avocado meal, soybean oil, lecithin, brewers dried yeast, flax seed, fish meal. No artificial colors, flavors, or preservatives.

Ground rice, soy flour, cracked pearl barley, canola oil, dicalcium phosphate, calcium carbonate, salt, carrots, choline chloride, garlic oil. Natural preservatives. No artificial colors or flavors.

Lamb meal, brewers rice, rice flour, cracked pearled barley, oat groats, ground wheat, corn gluten meal, animal fat, dried beet pulp, vegetable oil. Natural preservatives, no artificial colors or flavors.

Chicken meal, wheat flour, ground rice, lamb meal, poultry fat, ground wheat, dried whole eggs, lecithin, fish meal, brewers dried yeast. All natural preservatives, no artificial colors or flavors.

Lamb meal, rice, cracked pearled barley, oat groats, brewers dried yeast, dried beet pulp, lamb digest, animal fat, sunflower oil, salt. Preserved with BHA/BHT and potassium sorbate."

Lamb, rice flour, ground corn, fish meal, ground grain sorghum, dried egg product, dried beet pulp, animal fat, brewers dried yeast, dicalcium phosphate. Natural preservatives.

Chicken, chicken meal, ground brown rice, ground yellow corn, corn gluten meal, oatmeal, poultry fat, dried chicken liver, dried egg, dried kelp. Natural preservatives, no colors or flavors.

*** All foods listed here comply with AAFCO's requirements. However, this is the only food listed here that complies with AAFCO's "nutrient requirements" rather than the "feeding trials" protocol.*

*over 75 pounds need about 15% fewer calories per pound of body weight than those in the 20 to 75 pound range.*

■ ***Outside temperature****: If your dog spends most of his time outside, he'll probably need about 30% more calories in cold weather, from December through February than in the warmer months, June through August. A rule of thumb: with every 10 degree drop in temperature, dogs need about 7.5% more calories per day.*

■ ***Metabolism****: Dogs burn fat at different rates, just as humans do. Two dogs of similar size, age, and level of activity may need different amounts of food because of their metabolism. A nervous dog, a dog that moves in sudden bursts and a "high-energy" dog will very likely burn calories at a higher rate than their more sluggish compatriots.*

■ ***Neutering or spaying****: A neutered or spayed dog can become more docile and less nervous, and as a result may require fewer calories.* ❖

# 5

# Top 10 Dry Dog Foods

*What separates the great from the merely good?*
*Here are some criteria to help you*
*make your selection.*

There are countless pet food manufacturers calling their foods "premium" these days, but are you aware that the word doesn't actually mean anything? That is, there are no official standards a manufacturer has to meet in order to call its food "premium."

Unfortunately, countless dog owners are being taken in by this appellation—people who want "the best" for their dogs, and trust that a high price tag and the word "premium" on the label means they are buying the best food their Rovers could ever want.

In our view, in order to earn the title "premium," a food must be something really special. It's not enough to be simply un-awful; in our book, only foods that are formulated with the most wholesome, pure, and beneficial ingredients are "premium."

We've spent months examining the labels of all the best dry dog foods we could find, looking for truly healthy, top quality foods. Now we're ready to identify and describe our 10 favorites. Note that we've not seen *every* dog food on the market, because new foods pop up all the time, and some manufacturers market their products in regional areas only.

Along with our selections, we present the reasons we picked each food, so you can compare foods you are familiar with (but that do not appear here) and see for yourself what makes one better than the other.

Following are the criteria we used to make our selections. We chose foods that are made with:

■ Only the best sources of protein (whole, fresh meats or single-source meat, i.e. chicken meal rather than poultry meal, which may contain several types of fowl. Also, the use of any generic protein, i.e. "animal fat," disqualifies a food from our list).

■ No meat by-products (by-products in and of themselves are not necessarily evil. But these "second-class" products are not handled as carefully as whole meat. And the sources tend to be far more dubious than whole meat).

■ A whole-meat source as one of the first two ingredients (chicken or chicken meal, for instance, as opposed to chicken fat).

■ No artificial preservatives (including BHA, BHT, or ethoxyquin).

■ No artificial colors.

■ No sugars and sweeteners like corn syrup, sucrose, and ammoniated glycyrrhizin (added to attract dogs to otherwise unappealing food).

■ No propylene glycol (added to some foods to keep them moist).

# Embattled Ingredients

We've included corn, as long as the corn is presented in its whole, healthy form. Corn fragments (corn gluten meal, corn syrup, corn oil) do not qualify, especially if they appear high up in the ingredients list. (The ingredients are listed by weight. The more of something there is in the food, the higher it will appear on the list.)

Controversial corn? Oh yes; many foods are quite controversial in this highly competitive market, with manufacturers doing their very best to fan the flames in the direction of their rivals' ingredients. Take a look at how several different dog food makers have described corn:

■ **Beowulf's All Natural**: "Called the 'King of Carbohydrates,' corn readily metabolizes into usable energy and is a rich source of linoleic acid, and has a high level of digestibility."

■ **Flint River Ranch**: "Ordinary dog foods are made with corn. Rice and wheat are easier to digest than corn, and therefore easier on your dog's system."

■ **Canidae**: "No corn. No wheat. No soy."

We most respect the opinion of Natura Pet Products, who tells what appears to be – pardon us– the whole story:

"Ground corn is a good source of carbohydrates. And because it contains the entire kernel, it contributes additional protein, corn oil, corn bran, and vitamins and minerals to the diet. This is in contrast to corn fractions, which are leeched of many of these natural nutrients. The downside of corn is that it is a common allergen."

Manufacturers also argue about **beet pulp** ("cheap filler" vs. "good source of fiber") **wheat** ("the most common allergen" vs. "one of the most nutritionally balanced cereal grains"), **oven-baking vs. extrusion** ("oven-baking results in better nutrition" vs. "dry, wet, and steam-injected extrusion of ingredients maximizes nutritional value"), and even which type of **natural preservative** to use ("tocopherol works just fine as a preservative for up to 12 months" and "wholesome **vitamins C and E** offers all the properties of a chemical preservative without the associated health risks" vs. "vitamin E lasts only about a month as a preservative; vitamin C lasts only about 12 hours after the consumer opens the bag."

When caught in the crossfire, we've tried not to simply mouth the platitudes we've heard from one or two manufacturers; instead, we've used our own judgement to determine the validity of one opinion or another. We ask you to do the same. Check out our selections. Scrutinize the lists of ingredients. And by all means, analyze our arguments for our favorite foods.

# Top 10 Dry Dog Foods

■ **Back to Basics** (Chicken formula): Beowulf Natural Feeds is the radical in our group of dog food makers. Both their pork formula and their chicken formula (the latter is the one we recommend) are extremely high-fat foods; their Guaranteed Analysis states the fat content of both foods is 19%. This formulation stems from the founder's (a breeder of Mastiffs) belief that diets high in fat increase a dog's stamina and protect against heat stress. We will add that there is some compelling research that indicates that relatively higher-fat diets may benefit animals with cancer.

Besides the high fat content, another radical approach is offering a pork formula, which represents a departure from other dog food manufacturers. Because pork is more likely to contain parasites that can cause trichinosis, few, if any, other pet food manufacturers use pork. Beowulf claims to use only human grade pork, which would be unlikely to pose that risk. That sounds fine, but thanks, we'll just have the chicken.

The product literature says that the maker's goal is producing a highly digestible super premium food using natural, wholesome ingredients. Unlike other companies, this aim is consistent with Back to Basic's list of ingredients.

■ **California Natural**: This food is often recommended for dogs with allergies, due to the simplicity of the formulation; besides the requisite vitamin and mineral supplements, it contains only four ingredients. That simplifies matters when searching for a food with as few potential allergens as possible.

However, this high-quality food shouldn't be considered solely for allergic dogs. Think about it: If a food is "nutritionally complete," contains a good amount of protein and fat, and has only a few ingredients in it, those ingredients must be of the best quality.

■ **Canidae**: This is a nice food, loaded with great ingredients. Canidae claims to use nothing but Grade A lamb and Grade A poultry meal, and the only grains in the formula are whole brown and white rice. The food was formulated with an eye toward the ideal ration of Omega-3 and Omega-6 fatty acids (a 5-1 ratio), and has used good sources of Omega-3s (fish meal and flax seed). And though this could be considered "the kitchen sink" approach, Canidae has added herbs (rosemary and sage) and biotin for their beneficial effects on skin and hair.

■ **Flint River**: This is probably one of the best-known healthy dry dog foods available. Flint River's formulation of quality ingredients is not unique among premium foods, but its cooking method is different. The company oven bakes the food, rather than using the traditional "steam extrusion" technique. According to company literature, this form of cooking "changes the hard-to-digest molecules of 'raw' starches into easy-to-digest dextrines," resulting in "less strain on the dog's digestive system" and producing "a greater degree of food absorption." Like many manufacturers' claims, this is hard to prove. The proof, however, is in the pudding, and the people who feed Flint River uniformly rave about its positive effects on their dogs.

Wheat is a good food, and many dogs eat wheat without any ill effects. However, it is among a number of foods that some dogs are allergic to. Owners of wheat-allergic dogs, note that wheat is the second ingredient here.

■ **Innova**: Innova is the second food made by Natura that makes our Top 10 list, but our reasons for liking it are completely different than our reasons for liking California Natural.

This is another food taking the "kitchen sink" approach to feed formulation. Natura has included every conceivable food in Innova; though they are all good foods, it's impossible to know whether the tiny amounts of each ingredient are beneficial. Unlike most of the other foods, which tend to have the vitamins and minerals appearing shortly following the top 10 ingredients (if not before number 10), Innova continues with "whole steamed carrots, cottage cheese, sunflower oil, dicalcium phosphate (a source of calcium and phosphorus), alfalfa sprouts, whole eggs, garlic," and more. However, this is nitpicking. The first 10 ingredients are most important, and the ones here are winners.

■ **Limited Diet:** This food is uniquely qualified for our top 10 list. It's not a food you'd seek out for just any dog; it's specifically made for dogs with food allergies. However, this food, unlike the better-known Science Diet's allergy foods, contains better quality ingredients in its simple formulations (they offer two kinds: lamb and potato, and venison and potato). The only thing we don't like about this food is the use of "lamb digest," which is lamb meat and miscellaneous other lamb parts. But as the sixth ingredient, it's not a major constituent of this food.

■ **PetGuard LifeSpan:** This is a rather high protein food, with a high price. But the maker claims to use nothing but the best ingredients, including chicken raised without hormones. PetGuard's product literature says they freshly grind the grains used in LifeSpan on the first day of production, which helps keep the vitamins intact. PetGuard also claims to use a unique cooking method (one that goes undescribed) that "fully cooks the carbohydrates for better flavor, carbohydrate blending, and digestibility."

The one questionable ingredient here is corn gluten meal, which appears fifth on the list of ingredients. Corn gluten meal is a by-product from the manufacture of corn syrup.

■ **Pinnacle:** This is a fairly new offering from the people who produce Avo-Derm. This food, however, doesn't resemble that food in the least. If anything, the ingredients list looks more like Canidae's or Innova's than Avo-Derm's. It's in good company, anyway.

The list of ingredients looks great. We especially like the choice of foods used for carbo-

hyhydrates: oats, potatoes, quinoa, and vegetables. Using grapeseed oil for a source of fat is a unique choice, and this may well offer a dog who is allergic to fish or flaxseed oils another option.

The maker also included some probiotics in the formula. Experts argue whether probiotics can stay viable in a dry (or canned, for that matter) food, but it's a nice idea. So is the addition of rosemary nd sage extracts and biotin.

■ **Solid Gold**: This company has been criticized for monkeyshines regarding its labelling and its possibly overzealous claims about its

## DRY DOG FOOD INGREDIENTS

| Dog Food | Price/ Lb. | % Crude Protein | % Crude Fat | % Crude Fiber | Moisture |
|---|---|---|---|---|---|
| Back to Basics Chicken) | $1.00 | 23 | 19 | 10 | 10 |
| California Natural | $0.92 | 21 | 11 | 4.5 | 10 |
| Canidae | $0.75 | 24 | 14.5 | 4 | 18 |
| Flint River Chicken Meal & Rice Formula | $1.62 | 23 | 12 | 4 | 10 |
| Innova | $1.36 | 24 | 14 | 3 | 10 |
| Limited Diets | $1.48 | 19 | 10 | 4.5 | 10 |
| Pinnacle | $1.22 | 25 | 15 | 5 | 10 |
| Solid Gold | $1.00 | 22 | 8 | 5 | 10 |
| PetGuard LifeSpan | $1.20 | 26 | 15 | 4 | 12 |
| Wysong Maintenance | $1.00 | 24 | 12 | 4.3 | 12 |

*Note: All prices given are what we paid for the foods in the San Francisco Bay Area; prices in your area may be lower. Prices/Lb. rounded up to the nearest penny.*

potential benefits for dogs. However, no one has ever said the food is not good. Solid Gold has built a reputation for using top-quality ingredients, starting with USDA-inspected, hormone free lamb from New Zealand. Hund-N-Flocken, which means "dog food flakes" in German, contains none of the common allergens: no corn, no wheat, and no soybeans. In an interesting departure from many other manufacturers, Solid Gold disdains the use of chicken in its foods, citing the danger of salmonella poisoning, especially in chicken meat that has not been passed for human inspection. Hmmm.

**First 10 Ingredients**

Chicken meal, ground corn, chicken fat, oatmeal, long grain rice, dried tomato pomace, dried whole eggs, fish meal (herring), natural flavorings

Lamb meal, brown rice, rice, sunflower oil, vitamins & minerals.

Chicken meal, turkey meal, brown rice, white rice, lamb meal, poultry fat, fish meal, flax seed, alfalfa meal, sunflower oil

Chicken meal, wheat flour, ground rice, lamb meal,poultry fat, ground wheat, dried whole eggs, lecithin,fish meal, dried brewer's yeast

Turkey, chicken, chicken meal, whole ground. barley, whole ground. brown rice, whole steamed potatoes, ground. white rice, chicken fat, herring, whole raw apples

Potato, lamb, lamb meal, lamb fat, canola oil, lamb (Lamb) digest, (vitamins and minerals).

Chicken meal, whole ground. chicken, whole oat flour, toasted oats, tomato pomace, potato, chicken fat, quinoa, dehydrated mixed vegetables, grapeseed oil

Lamb meal, ground whole millet, ground brown rice, ground whole barley, amaranth, menhaden fish meal, rice oil, canola oil, flaxseed oil, garlic

Chicken, chicken meal, ground brown rice, ground yellow corn, corn gluten meal, oatmeal, poultry fat, dried chicken liver, dried whole egg

Chicken, chicken meal, ground. brown rice, ground. yellow corn, corn gluten meal, oatmeal, poultry fat, ground.whole soybeans, corn gluten meal, salt, dried kelp

■ **Wysong**: Like Solid Gold, Wysong was built on the reputation of its quality ingredients. The company's founder, veterinarian R. L. Wysong, is a driven individual, and healthy foods are his lifeblood. He's written a number of books, has produced videos, and might even, for all we know, have songs about the importance of "health-optimizing ingredients" including things like whole grains, free-range chickens, and active enzymes and probiotic cultures.

Wysong was one of the first pet food makers to package his products in specially sealed bags to keep the food free of light and oxygen until it's opened. The "Nutri-Paks" keep the food fresh and prevent the growth of mold and bacteria.

Wysong is also one of the few food manufacturers to encourage dog owners to feed fresh, whole foods in addition to dry food. One brochure reasonably states, "No one would consent to feeding themselves or their children only one processed, packaged food for a lifetime...to never eat fresh, natural foods for humans is no more appropriate than it is for pets who have even more recently been removed from the wild." Hurrah for Dr. Wysong – and his quality foods.

# Dry-Matter Math

*The guaranteed analysis on a bag of dog food says "not less than 25 percent protein," but the analysis on a can of dog food says "not less than 10 percent protein." How do you make an "apples to apples" protein comparison? Here's how:*

■ *Convert the as-fed percentages listed on the bag and can to dry-matter (waterless) percentages to account for the fact that canned foods contain up to 78 percent moisture, while dry foods usually contain only 10 percent moisture.*

■ *Calculate the dry-matter nutrient content of both foods by subtracting the moisture content from 100:*
*Dry:       100 minus 10=90% dry-matter content;*
*Canned:    100 minus 78 = 22% dry-matter content;*

■ *Determine the dry-matter percentage of protein by multiplying the as-fed protein content by 100 and dividing by the dry-matter content:*

> *Dry: 25 x 100 ÷ 90 = 27.8% protein (dry-matter basis)*
> *Canned: 10 x 100 ÷ 22 = 45.5% protein (dry-matter basis)*
>
> *Conclusion: Canned food contains a higher percentage of protein than dry. You can do similar conversions for other nutrients listed in the guaranteed analysis.*

# Pesticides in Food:
# In There Somewhere

There isn't a pet food label in the world that lists pesticides as an ingredient, but that doesn't mean there aren't any in the bag or box. Food inspectors can tell you that a small percentage of all grains, fruits, vegetables, and meats do contain some pesticides. Every commercially farmed food not labeled as "organic" (and even some of those) is exposed to pesticides at some point in its production.

The FDA's Center for Food Safety and Applied Nutrition (CFSAN) conducts annual testing to monitor pesticide-residue levels in human foods and animal feed, and establishes "acceptable" residue levels. In 1998, the CFSAN tested 482 domestic and 60 imported feed samples (presumably for all species). Of the samples tested, 39.2 percent of the domestic feeds and 38.3 percent of the imported feeds contained detectable pesticide residues; 1.7 percent of the domestics and 5 percent of the imports had levels that **exceeded** the FDA's regulatory guidelines. The domestic samples alone contained 295 different identifiable residues, though most of those (64.1 percent) were of the pesticides malathion, chlorpyrifos-methyl, and diazinon.

It's well-known that pesticide residues at levels that exceed FDA guidelines certainly can pose a health hazard. But some holistic health experts feel that even the tiny "allowable" doses of pesticides that people and their pets "take" with their food on a daily basis can contribute to poor health. Anna Maria Scholey, MA Vet.MB, MRCVS, who operates the holistic PetSynergy practice in Carrollton, Texas (and the Web site of the same name), believes that "it is far better to feed organic whole-grain feed" grown with no pesticides whatsoever.

Our dogs are exposed to a lot of toxins in their short lifetimes – flea control products, heartworm preventatives, pesticides and herbicides on grass, rug and floor cleaners, and annual vaccinations for umpteen diseases, to name a few. It just makes sense to try to reduce their exposure to whichever toxins you can. Buy organic whenever you can—for yourself, your family, and your canine companions. ❀

# 6

# Top 10 Canned Foods

*Finding the best canned dog food
for your pooch can be difficult;
but the end result is worth it.*

D og food is a big deal. This is partly because it's so important (all dogs eat food), and partly because it's so complex. Regulation of the pet food industry in this country is spotty at best. Enforcement of what rules there are is practically non-existent. And nutritionists continue to argue among themselves about what dogs need.

Educating ourselves about what our dogs are eating is important. It's also difficult. The pet food industry is not accustomed to scrutiny; many manufacturers feel it is simply not in their best interests to reveal everything about their foods. And because the best foods are usually made by small companies with smaller advertising budgets, it can be hard to locate their products. We'll start by telling you what kind of foods go into dog foods.

No one should ever have to see the making of sausage or laws, someone once said. Perhaps we ought to add the making of dog food to that list. The more you know about this industry, the more you want to make an appointment with your friendly neighborhood grocery store butcher, to discuss the best and most affordable cuts of meats for dogs. Because meat, as anyone who knows anything about optimum nutrition for dogs will tell you, is the food that all diets for dogs should be constructed around. (If your dog is allergic to meat he is the exception, not the rule.)

But it is inconvenient and expensive to buy, store, and prepare meat. And because dogs are considered omnivores (they eat meat and plant materials), not true carnivores (animals that eat only meat), you need to supplement their diets with bits of this and that to satisfy their nutritional needs.

And, if there's anything humans hate, it's inconvenience and expense, so an entire multi-billion-dollar industry has sprung up to make feeding our dogs easier.

Thanks to the dog food companies, we can take care of our dog's needs by just ripping open a paper bag, or getting out the old can opener and spooning a bunch of glop into a bowl—and Fido is fed—quickly and efficiently.

## CANNED DOG FOOD INGREDIENTS

| Dog Food | Price/Oz. | % Crude Protein | % Crude Fat | % Crude Fiber | Moisture |
|---|---|---|---|---|---|
| Breeder's Choice Avo Lamb & Rice | $0.07 | 8.5 | 8 | 1.5 | 78 |
| Solid Gold Chicken, Liver, Brown Rice | $0.07 | 8.0 | 4.0 | 1.0 | 78 |
| Hi-Tor Eno-Diet | $0.07 | 6.5 | 3 | 0.5 | 74 |
| California Natural Lamb & Rice Formula | $0.08 | 9 | 6 | 1.5 | 74 |
| Canidae | $0.08 | 9 | 6 | 1.5 | 78 |
| Innova | $0.08 | 9 | 6 | 1.5 | 74 |
| Wysong Maintenance | $0.09 | 7 | 4 | 1 | 75 |
| Neura 95 Natural 95% Beef | $0.10 | 9 | 5 | 1 | 78 |
| Petguard Beef & Chunky Dinner | $0.13 | 8 | 4 | 2 | 76 |
| Spot's Stew | $0.17 | 3.5 | 1.5 | 1.5 | 85 |

Note: All prices given are what we paid for the foods in the San Francisco Bay Area; prices in your area may be different. Foods are arranged alphabetically by price.

And we paid less for that glop, in most cases, than we would have for fresh meat. So what's the problem?

The problem is, our dogs are suffering from a multitude of allergies, illnesses and disorders. They develop cancers of every conceivable description. They have trouble reproducing, and they die young. They itch all over, their eyes drip, their ears exude wax, they smell awful, they have diarrhea, they have constipation.

Could this have anything to do with the food they eat every day?

Well, let's look at their food. What's in this stuff, anyway?

**First 10 Ingredients**

Lamb, lamb broth, brown rice, whole egg, flaxseed, avocado oil, lecithin, dried kelp, vegetable gum, potassium chloride.

Chicken, liver, ground brown rice, ground barley, garlic, sesame oil, vitamin A supplement, choline chloride, niacin, vitamin E supplement.

Water, chicken, rice, liver, whole egg, corn meal, cottage cheese, dicalcium phosphate, guar gum, salt.

Lamb, spring water, brown rice, rice, sunflower oil, flaxseed, vegetable gums, dl-alpha tocopherol, dicalcium phosphate, sodium ascorbate.

Chicken, chicken broth, lamb, chicken liver, ocean fish, brown rice, sun cured alfalfa, egg, sunflower oil, lecithin.

Turkey, chicken, spring water, potatoes, brown rice, chicken fat, eggs, apples, carrots, cottage cheese.

Chicken, water SFP, ground brown rice, ground corn, ground extruded whole soybeans, carrots, barley, bone meal, dicalcium phosphate, whole egg.

Beef, beef broth, rice flour, guar gum, onion powder, salt, carrageenan gum, potassium chloride, choline chloride, ferrous sulfate.

Coleman Natural Beef, chicken, soy flour, liver, water SFP, potatoes, peas, carrots, ground corn, wheat germ.

Water SFP, chicken, carrots, celery, yellow squash, zucchini, chicken liver, green beans, green peas, pasta.

# Second-class Food

It shouldn't be a surprise to anyone that dogs eat the stuff that we won't – parts of animal carcasses that we think are unappetizing, like bones, brains, blood, intestines, and ligaments. After all, wild dogs eat absolutely every part of the animals they eat – the parts that offer lots of quality nutrients, as well as the parts with lesser amounts of nutrients. But many people are unaware that unless a dog food says it contains "meat," it contains only the parts of animal carcasses that are of minimal use to the dog. Highly processed "meat by-products," "animal fat," "meat and bone meal," offer almost no nutrition to the dogs that eat them. **That's why we would never recommend any dog food that contains any meat "by-products."**

---

...OUR DOGS ARE SUFFERING FROM A MULTITUDE OF ALLERGIES, ILLNESSES AND DISORDERS...COULD THIS HAVE ANYTHING TO DO WITH THE FOOD THEY EAT EVERY DAY?

---

But even products that utilize the "best" parts of animal carcasses – the more nutritious, choice cuts of muscle tissue and fat from chicken and other poultry, beef, lamb, and fish – are second rate, compared to what humans eat. Not just meat discards are fed to our dogs. We also give them the discards from our grain and vegetable industries! Corn starch, wheat gluten, beet pulp, tomato pomace – these are the parts of the plants that aren't used in human foods. It's little wonder that most of the gigantic processed human food companies own pet-food subsidiaries: no waste!

Then, to make up for the low-quality foods and for the loss of almost all the food's nutrients due to processing, the manufacturers add vitamins and minerals. Without this supplementation, the food would be useless to its consumers.

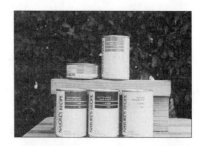

# Canned Food Considerations

But if you can't or won't make your dogs' food yourself, and yet want your dog to eat the best food you can buy, the task is finding products with the best-quality ingredients. This means whole foods, not just cast-off parts of foods. It also means meats that are human-grade. Obviously, this means the food is going to be more expensive than food made of what is essentially garbage.

Canned foods have a few inherent advantages and disadvantages. A dog who eats nothing but canned food, even if it is of the very best quality available, will require access to additional foods, treats, and/or toys that offer enough abrasive action to clean their teeth and exercise their gums. Canned food is also expensive. For these reasons, few experts, if any, recommend feeding nothing but canned food. Most suggest that canned food be offered to dogs as a "top dressing" on kibble.

On the plus side, despite the common perception that canned foods are chemical soups, they actually contain way fewer chemical additives than dry foods. Artificial colors and flavors are uncommon in the better foods, and much less common in the worst foods than they are in their dried food equivalents. Preservatives are unnecessary and rarely seen, due to the sealed, oxygen-free environment that a can offers. (Because of the lack of preservatives, however, canned foods *must* be kept refrigerated after opening, just like any other meat. And if a dog doesn't finish all of his canned food immediately, the food must be discarded. Harmful bacteria can quickly develop in meat-based foods that linger at room temperature.)

The most common chemical additives in canned food are stabilizers, emulsifiers, and thickening agents. These include carrageenan gum, guar gum, vegetable gum, potassium chloride, dicalcium phosphate, and calcium carbonate.

Most other ominous-sounding chemicals are vitamin and mineral sources. Some of the most commonly seen include: choline chloride, a dietary supplement in the B complex; ferrous sulfate, a nutritional iron source; manganese oxide, a nutritional manganese source; and calcium pantothenate, a B-complex vitamin.

# Canned Food Selection Criteria

■ *No artificial colors, flavors, or preservatives*

■ *No meat and bone meal*

■ *No meat by-products (This requirement is what was respon- sible for eliminating popular brands such as Iams, Waltham, Science Diet, Excel, and Abacus.)*

■ *A quality, whole meat listed in the top two ingredients (in canned foods, water is usually the first or second ingredient)*

■ *All whole foods, not a hodgepodge of reconstituted parts, i.e. "rice," rather than "rice flour, rice bran, brewers rice," etc. (This is what eliminated Nutro and NutroMax brands).*

# Top 10 Canned Dog Foods

These are not ranked, but listed from least to most expensive; when their prices are the same, they are listed alphabetically.

■ **Breeder's Choice Avo-Derm**: The use of lamb broth instead of water is a nutritional plus. The maker is particularly forthcoming about the sources of his ingredients, always a good sign of quality.

■ **Solid Gold**: How did they manage to make a canned food without added water for processing? We don't know, but what this means to us is that we're paying for food. And it's good food!

■ **Hi-Tor Eno Diet**: With water in the first position on the label, you should expect the reduced protein level. But the ingredients are better than average.

■ **California Natural**: A simple, short ingredients list, plus the maker's guarantee that only human-grade foods are used. Hard to beat.

■ **Canidae**: A relative newcomer, Canidae can be hard to find, but is worth the effort, with several quality protein sources and chicken broth replacing water. (800) 398-1600.

■ **Innova**: An attractive-looking food, with identifiable contents. Nice ingredients list for the dog who likes veggies with his meat.

■ **Wysong Maintenance**: The only food we examined that didn't smell like dog food! In fact, it looks and smells yummy. The maker is devoted to quality ingredients.

■ **Neura 95** (95% Beef): One of the six varieties sold under this label, the "95% Beef" is guaranteed to be 95% beef. Watch out for our "not recommended" ingredients in the other five.

■ **Petguard** (with Coleman Beef): The only dog food we've ever seen with certified organic beef. Top-notch food.

■ **Spot's Stew**: This is wildly expensive food that we wouldn't mind eating for dinner – seriously. The maker guarantees all ingredients are human-grade. If you want only the best, and price is no object, this is it. A new, hard-to-find product. ❧

# 7

# The Dog "Zone"

*Whether you make it or buy it,*
*customize the ratio of proteins, fats, and*
*carbohydrates to suit your dog.*

The Zone Diet... Dr. Barry Sears' thoughts on diet have swept the world. Movie stars and NBA players have proclaimed it miraculous. Books, magazines, and TV shows are spreading the word: Eat in "The Zone," and you'll lose excess weight, feel better, and live longer.

Briefly, Dr. Sears theories culminate in a simple prescription for the ideal human diet: Each of our daily meals (and, hence, our total diet) should be comprised of 30 percent protein, 30 percent fat, and 40 percent carbohydrates.

The Zone diet has been roundly criticized by other nutritionists, who contend that Sears' high-protein diet can tax the kidneys, and that any weight loss that a person may experience with the diet is from a simple reduction in consumed calories, not from some sort of "magic ratio" of nutrients.

## Crossover Diet Ideas

The fuss over The Zone diet made us wonder: Is there a canine "Zone"? What is the ideal ratio of protein, fat, and carbohydrates for dogs?

Celeste Yarnall, PhD, animal nutritionist and author of the 1998 book, *Natural Dog Care*, concurs with Sears regarding several integral aspects of Zone dieting. In fact, Yarnall consulted with Sears when preparing her recommendations for canine diets, and feels that Sears' "Zone" ratio of 30 percent protein, 30 percent fat, and 30 percent carbohydrates is a healthy prescription for canine diets.

However, our opinion is that there are not just one, but several healthy dog "zones," primarily because there a number of factors determine the percentages of protein, fat, and carbohydrates – as well as the micro-nutrient levels – in any given dog's diet. The dog's age, size, state of health, work load, and environment should all be taken into consideration in determining his diet.

# Proteins, Fats & Carbs

For starters, owners need to learn what function each type of macronutrient serves in their dog's food, and to understand what their dog needs, based on his age, breed, health, and activity level. We start with the **macronutrients (protein, fat, and carbo-hydrates)**, and then proceed to the **micronutrients (vitamins and minerals)** later.

Every commercial dog food maker includes **macronutrients – proteins, fats, and carbohydrates** – in varying percentages in their products. But in recent years, some companies have begun formulating dog foods with higher percentages of protein and/or fat.

While there is no regulated definition of the word "premium," many of the companies who make high-protein or high-fat foods call these products "premium" foods, and tout them as more healthful for dogs than typical grocery store offerings. What is responsible for the move to higher fats and/or proteins in canine diets?

Just as with the field of human nutrition, waves of popular theory tend to sweep across the field of animal nutrition every few years. In the last 15 years or so, nutritionists have become occupied with the idea that the modern diet may be responsible for current levels of the major diseases seen in modern humans – cardiovascular disease, cancer, diabetes, etc. A return to a diet modeled more along the lines of Paleolithic man, some nutritionists speculate, might result in less disease.

Following this line of thought, some veterinary nutritionists theorize that many of our dogs' ills have stemmed from their modern-day commercial diets, which have evolved more out of regard for the needs of food manufacturers' and dog owners than the needs of dogs. Given that, genetically, our dogs are not much different from the dogs of Paleolithic times, putting them on a pre-domestication diet might be one part of restoring canine health to robustness.

# Proteins Pros and Cons

The amount of beneficial protein in a food can similarly depart from the stated level on the food's label. The American Association of Feed Control Officials (AAFCO) requires dog food makers to list only the crude protein contained in the food on the label, rather than the digestible protein. While some companies – generally the ones with higher-quality proteins in their foods – voluntarily list the amount of digestible protein in their foods, this is the exception, rather than the rule. Regardless of which fat/protein/carbohydrate ratio you are shooting for, determining the protein portion provided by your dog's favorite food may require a little detective work.

Protein quality is judged by the protein's digestibility and amino acid levels. The higher the biologic value of a protein, the less the amount of that protein needed in a diet to meet all of an animal's essential amino acid requirements.

Because most proteins extracted from plant or grain sources are low in certain amino acids, most commercial foods combine animal tissues, cereal grains, and sometimes, soybean meal, to ensure a balance of complementary amino acids. Soy protein is nutritionally equivalent or superior to animal protein, providing high levels of most essential amino acids. When fed in combination with complementary sources of essential fatty acids, soy can provide excellent protein nutrition.

Meat protein sources should be as complete and wholesome as possible. The more processing that a meat is put through, the fewer vital nutrients it will contain. Vitamins and vital enzymes deteriorate with exposure to oxygen and with heat, so look for foods with turkey, beef, lamb, or chicken (preferably in the first three ingredients). Several big steps lower on the quality scale are products that contain turkey, beef, lamb, or chicken meal, which are ground, processed products. Several steps lower are foods that contain generic mixtures of several types of animal products, euphemistically called "poultry meal," or worse, "meat meal."

According to Dr. Strombeck, protein sources are the most likely ingredients in commercially prepared dog foods to be unwholesome. According to most holistic veterinary practitioners, home-preparing your dog's food with top-quality protein sources is the only way to guarantee the digestibility and usefulness of the protein.

In particular, older dogs can benefit from higher percentages of protein (and higher quality protein), largely because they are less efficient at processing the proteins.

However, total dietary protein should be restricted for dogs with chronic kidney disease, since processing protein exacts a toll on the kidneys. Protein should also be reduced for dogs in recovery from acute pancreatitis, since protein can trigger pancreatic secretion. The small amount of protein that is fed to these dogs, then, should be of the highest quality possible.

# Life In the Fat Lane

Most veterinary nutritional literature recommends a range of five to 20 percent fat for most dogs. Sears' Zone Diet (and Yarnall's identical recommended ratio of proteins, fats, and carbohydrates for dogs) contain considerably more fat (and more protein) than most dogs who eat commercially prepared foods (without additional supplementation) generally receive. There are a number of dogs who can benefit, in our opinion, from high-fat diets. In particular, super-athletes (dogs who pull sleds, hunt extensively, run long distance with their owners, etc.) can benefit from a higher percentage of fat in their diets. In order to perform these strenuous activities, these dogs require more total calories than their sedentary brethren; a high percentage of fat in the active dog's diet seems to provide the additional calories thanks to a uniquely efficient process called "fat adaptation," a process whereby the body "learns," over time, to break down and utilize dietary fats especially effectively.

Hilary Watson, an Alaskan dog sledder and a major proponent of high-fat diets, explains: "A high-fat diet, in conjunction with endurance training, causes cardiovascular, pulmonary, and enzymatic changes that enhance the ability to use fatty acids as fuel for muscle activity. This is known as 'fat adaptation.'"

Stresses (from physical exertion, to environmental or psychological stress) increase a dog's requirement for energy as well as non-energy nutrients. High-stress or -performance diets should be high in metabolizable energy, which a high fat content can help provide. Fat is high in energy density and digestibility, providing about 2.5 times more energy than any other nutrient. Working dogs exposed to a variety of stressful situations including racing, hunting, police duty, guiding, and extensive showing, as well as dogs that experience extreme ambient temperatures, would especially benefit from higher-fat diets.

The importance of diet in one form of stress, such as exhaustive physical activity, is emphasized by a 1980 study in which four diets (three commercial and one experimental) were compared by the endurance performance of Beagle dogs on a treadmill. Digestible fat intake was positively correlated with endurance performance, but there was no significant association between digestible protein intake and performance. Carbohydrate content was also varied in the diets associated with these endurance tests, but results were inconclusive.

To feed for weather extremes such as Arctic temperatures, sled dog handlers must increase their dogs' rations; wind chill factors in open areas can increase the dogs' energy needs by 70-80 percent!

Dietary energy needs also increase with high temperatures and humidity. Tropical climates increase the calories expended for cooling, and reduce the dog's desire to eat, so more calories are required in fewer grams of diet.

Especially large active breeds of dogs may also benefit from diets with higher percentages of fat. These dogs may need extra calories to maintain adequate body weight. Dogs who have cancer can also benefit from a diet containing a high percentage of fat. Of particular importance is that dogs with cancer NOT receive diets high in carbohydrates; recent data from studies by leading canine cancer researcher Dr. Gregory K. Ogilvie of the Colorado State University, Fort Collins, School of Veterinary Medicine, suggest that cancer thrives on carbohydrates.

# Cancer Considerations

The one worry about feeding a high-fat diet to dogs – including dogs with cancer – is that the fat will make them feel full before they have eaten enough food to meet their needs for vital calories and micronutrients. "If the percentage of dietary fat is too high, the dog will stop eating before he has met his nutritional requirements, which can cause a nutritional deficiency to develop," warns Donald R. Strombeck, DVM, Ph.D., Professor Emeritus at the University of California at Davis School of Veterinary Medicine, author of the 1999 book, *Home-Prepared Dog and Cat Diets.*

For this reason, Dr. Strombeck recommends that anyone who feeds their dog a high-fat diet ensure that the food sources are of the highest quality. A highly digestible, nutrient-dense food is especially important for canine cancer patients, who may have a poor appetite; what little food they eat should be as nutritionally beneficial as possible, not full of "empty" calories.

There isn't much agreement among veterinary nutritionists regarding high-fat diets for ordinary dogs. "No one knows the cardiovascular effects of feeding a high-fat diet over long periods of time to average dogs," cautions Marty Fettman, DVM, of the Colorado State University, Fort Collins, School of Veterinary Medicine. "Feeding trials must be generational in length before we can judge the costs or benefits of feeding such a diet to dogs."

There are a few cases where it might be helpful to restrict a dog's dietary fat. Dogs who frequently suffer diarrhea may benefit from a lower-fat diet.

Interestingly, EFA deficiencies also can occur in dog who receive foods that are manufactured with adequate fat. This can happen when the EFAs are oxidized due to over-long storage or poor storage (warm or humid) conditions. Avoid buying pet food that has been stored too long (and has suffered some degradation of its ingredients), and buy from retail outlets with high turnover, or direct from the manufacturer. Buy only enough food to feed your pet for a month to six weeks, to ensure freshness. Store bags in the refrigerator or freezer, or at least a cool dry place to keep oils from rancidity.

# Carbohydrate Controversies

Carbohydrates are the main source of energy for all body functions and are needed to process other nutrients. Plants make carbohydrates as a product of photosynthesis, storing the carbon-based substances in their leaves, stems, roots, and fruits. Our bodies can also produce certain carbohydrates.

Fruits are often more than 90 percent carbohydrate, usually in the sweet-tasting simple form of glucose and fructose. Green and yellow vegetables store most of their calories as complex carbohydrates (containing a large number of glucose molecules), but contain few total calories.

Whole grains (rice and corn), the whole grain flours (wheat, rye), tubers (potatoes, yams), and legumes (beans, peas), contain large amounts of complex carbohydrates. Rice, corn, and other grains (along with potatoes), store about 80 percent of their calories in the form of these complex carbohydrates. Beans, peas, and lentils are about 70 percent complex carbohydrates.

Carbohydrates are digested by enzymes in the small intestine or the gut. Most of the carbohydrates in dog foods are broken down and absorbed as glucose or other simple sugars before being used for energy.

Carbohydrates are classified into two groups based on their solubility (digestibility): Dietary soluble carbohydrates supply relatively inexpensive calories (3.5 kilocalories/gram). Dietary insoluble carbohydrates (fiber) provide no significant energy to the dog.

Most commercial dog foods include either corn, wheat, rice, or any number of combinations of these grains in their products, largely because these foods are less expensive than other sources of dietary energy and certain nutrients. This means that most commercial dog foods contain high percentages of carbohydrates relative to the amount of protein and fat. But despite the pet food industry's reliance on grains, there is quite a bit of controversy as to whether dogs need or should even have carbohydrates. Neither the National Research Council (NRC) nor AAFCO makes recommendations for a dog's carbohydrate daily requirement.

Canine (and feline) nutrition specialist Celeste Yarnall and "Zone Diet " developer Barry Sears agree on the ideal "Zone" ratio for dogs, and concur that humans and hounds alike eat way too many carbohydrates. One of the most obvious differences between the diet of today's domesticated dog and the ancestral diet of the wild dog is the heavy consumption of carbohydrate-laden grains.

Insoluble carbohydrates (fiber) tend to pass right through the animal. Diets high in fiber may be appropriate for dogs who tend to eat too much, since fiber absorbs water on its way through the digestive tract, which helps lend a feeling of fullness to the bored or food-obsessed dog.

High-fiber diets are inappropriate for dogs that have high energy requirements (growth, late gestation, lactation, stress, work), as fiber has been shown to decrease the absorption of nutrients and displace useful energy sources. Excessive dietary fiber is also associated with adverse effects such as the production of loose stools and flatulence. You may notice a proliferation of looser stools when feeding foods containing lots of fiber; this may include so-called "lite" foods, formulated for the aforementioned bored and obese dog.

Interestingly, studies have shown that both adult dogs and puppies (after weaning) can grow and thrive on diets containing almost no carbohydrates whatsoever – an astonishing fact, considering that some commercial dog foods (especially the most inexpensive brands) contain this macronutrient in excess of 60 percent.

As Dr. Strombeck reminds us, "You can expect that the least expensive dog foods will be largely comprised of cereal, and offer poor palatability and digestibility. ...You get what you pay for." ❧

# 8

# Essential EFAs

*A lack of Essential Fatty Acids
in the canine diet can contribute to disease.*

Most animal lovers know that dogs need high quality protein, fat, and a complete complement of vitamins and minerals in their diet to remain healthy. We know that the foods our canine companions eat should come from clean, wholesome sources, and that a good diet must be combined with ample exercise and a healthy living environment. But when planning a diet for a companion animal, many of us overlook some very important aspects of what constitutes complete nutrition for our pet. In fact, some important nutritional elements are omitted from the diets of millions of dogs, contributing to chronic disease and perhaps even premature death.

Selecting the proper type and quality of food for our dogs is just a start. We also must be assured that the foods we select actually contain the nutritional values that are needed, and that these values are delivered to the body in a form that can be readily absorbed and properly metabolized.

There are many factors that interfere with nutritional quality of pet foods.

■ First, we must consider that many pet foods are comprised of ingredients that are of a much lower quality than humans demand, and lower quality foods are more difficult for an animal to digest and assimilate.

■ Second, we must consider that even the best brands of commercial pet foods (and many home-prepared diets) are prepared at

high temperatures, meaning that many of the nutritional components they once contained are destroyed before they reach the food
bowl.

■ Third, we have to consider the effects of oxidation in com-
mercially-prepared pet foods – especially kibble.

Many important nutritional components of dried kibble begin to
degrade shortly after the food is manufactured, and often the food
will sit in a warehouse for months before even reaching the retail-
er. Because of this, the discriminating animal guardian should never
assume that everything on a pet food label still exists in the bag at
the time of purchase.

# EFAs Are Especially Important

Topping the list of things commonly missing from the companion
animal diet are essential fatty acids (EFAs). EFAs are fat-carried nutrients that every mammal needs to maintain healthy function and
structure of smooth muscle organs (i.e. heart, reproductive system),
to protect and build liver cells, and to maintain healthy skin, coat,
and strong joint tissues.

They have also been linked to retinal development and antioxidant activities, and they are responsible for the synthesis and mod-
ulation of various prostaglandins – chemicals that serve as mediators
of various physiologic processes in the body.

Most notably, prostaglandins act upon smooth muscle contrac-
tions of the heart and digestive tract, the initiation and regulation
of inflammatory responses, and serve to inhibit excessive clotting
of the blood.

In other words, if a body (animal or human) does not receive sufficient amounts of EFAs, critical body functions can be severely dis-
rupted. Dogs and cats that are deficient of EFAs typically develop
chronic skin and coat disorders, digestive problems, cardiovascular disease, degenerative eye disease, and allergies.

Even animals who show no obvious signs of chronic disease will
usually display dramatic benefits of an EFA-enriched diet very quickly. A shinier and softer coat, less shedding, healthier skin, fewer
fleas, and better tolerance to flea bites and other allergens can be
seen within just a few weeks of first feeding a top-quality EFA supplement.

With all of this in mind, it's easy to understand why EFAs should
not be regarded as supplemental measures of nutrition, but as fun-
damental components of good health.

# Omega-3 and Omega-6

Scientists categorize EFAs into two general groups. The first (alpha-linolenic acid) comprises the Omega-3 fatty acids, which are derived mostly from animal fats but also from flax seed oil (the richest source) and a few other vegetable oils. The second (linoleic acid) comprises Omega-6 fatty acids, which are available from many vegetable sources, most notably the seed oils of borage, evening primrose, and black current.

It's just as important for the ratio of Omega-6 to Omega-3 EFAs to be correct as it is for dogs to have them in their diets. A ratio of about 4-1 Omega-6 to Omega-3 is considered optimum for dogs. Many commercial dog foods contain EFAs in ratios of 20-1; ratios of 50-1 or more (often seen in foods that contain lots of corn, which contains high levels of Omega-6 EFAs) will result in an Omega-3 deficiency.

All sources of EFAs are very unstable, meaning they tend to oxidize and break down very quickly, and are destroyed by heat, light, and oxygen. This is where our pet food problem begins.

The cooking of food (or canned food sterilizing) destroys the critical EFAs our animals need, and exposure to air breaks them down and renders them useless very quickly. Fish oils (an excellent source of Omega 3 fatty acids) are the fastest to go rancid. The oxidation and subsequent EFA degradation of flax seed, borage seed, evening primrose seed, or black currant seed oil occurs more slowly, but nevertheless, these oils cannot be expected to remain viable for more than a few months – especially if the oil is exposed to oxygen (which, in a bottled or powdered supplement, can happen every evening at the dog's meal time).

EFA supplements are often provided in the form of a bottled oil mixture that is added to the dog's food daily in small amounts. But in the few weeks or months it can take to use a bottle of oil, the EFA content will progressively diminish. By the time half of a four- to eight-ounce bottle is gone, we will only be able to guess how much essential fatty acid is actually left.

While they sound like a great idea, EFA-fortified commercial foods are not a reliable source of EFAs. Not only are most prepared with heat (which can destroy naturally-occurring EFAs), they are also subject to oxidation. Even vacuum-packaged dry foods contain oxygen within each kibble, and there is no way of telling how much EFA remains in the food at the time of purchase, much less after the substance sits in an opened bag for several days.

The bottom line is this: the only way you can assure that your canine companion is getting sufficient amounts of EFAs is to add an EFA supplement to your dog's diet yourself, using a guaranteed-fresh source packaged in an oxygen-free container.

We like the Animal Essentials Essential Fatty Acid Supplement produced by Merritt Naturals (See Appendix). This formula provides a diverse and balanced complement of EFAs as well as additional nutritional factors that promote healthy blood and skin structure. Best of all, they have contained the oils in convenient, easy-to-open soft gel capsules that prohibit air from contacting the formula until the feeding time. This optimizes shelf life of the product and helps assure that your companion actually receives the essential fatty acids he needs.

# Requirements and Dosages

No exact requirements of these supplements have been established as yet. Exactly how of much of each type of essential fatty acid a particular animal needs remains questionable, but most experts agree that dogs need a balance of both Omega-3 and Omega-6 acids in their diets. Some EFAs are synthesized within an animal's body, while others must be derived exclusively from dietary sources. EFA requirements may also vary according to animal type. For example, dogs can produce arachidonic acid (an important EFA component) whereas cats cannot. Instead, cats must receive arachidonic acid directly from their diets. Animal fats, evening primrose oil, and borage seed oil are all good sources of arachidonic acid.

Because the dietary needs and metabolic rates of EFA absorption vary between the type of oil and the systemic variations of each individual animal, it is best to feed EFAs from a variety of fish and vegetable seed oil sources. A commonly accepted dosage is about 400-600 mg. of the combined oils, fed daily for each 20 pounds of a dog's body weight (e.g., a 60-pound dog would require 1200-1800 mg.) ❧

# 9

# Converting to a Raw Diet

*The whys and hows of making the
switch to raw foods. There's a growing trend
away from packages and cans.*

For thousands of years, Mother Nature has fed her dogs and cats raw food. Their wild cousins continue to dine on freshly captured prey, but most American dogs and cats eat commercial pet foods from cans and packages or home-cooked grains and meats.

The result, say a number of veterinarians and nutritionists, is deteriorating health in our canine companions. In response is a growing trend toward home-prepared diets for our dogs, away from cooked food and toward more natural fare.

While commercial pet food companies developed and promoted their product lines in the 1940s and 50s, Afghan Hound breeder Juliette de Bairacli Levy fed her dogs raw meat, raw bones, raw goat's milk, raw fish, raw eggs, and a variety of raw fruits, vegetables, nuts, and oils. Supremely healthy and intelligent, her dogs won numerous championships. De Bairacli Levy described her "Natural Rearing" philosophy in a series of books, and gained a devoted following around the world.

Australian veterinarian Ian Billinghurst has converted many dog owners to raw food with his books *Give Your Dog a Bone* and *Feed Your Pups with Bones.* His well-known BARF diet (Bones and Raw Foods, or Biologically Appropriate Raw Foods) consists of raw meaty bones, occasional raw eggs or ripe fruit, small amounts of raw pureed vegetables, and other extras, such as kelp, herbs, and table scraps. Billinghurst does not use cooked grains, explaining that they contain relatively poor quality protein, interfere with calcium absorption, stress the pancreas, and contribute to mineral imbalances, allergies, and diabetes.

# Making the Switch

Although some dog owners have switched from cooked to raw in a single day without incident, such a drastic change can trouble some dogs. Here are some common-sense guidelines that help dogs and owners make a smooth transition to a new diet.

First, change your dog's feeding schedule. This is especially important if you've been leaving food out all day. In the wild, dogs hunt when they're hungry, gorge themselves when they catch prey, and go hunting again on an empty stomach. No animal in the wild lounges beside a food dispenser.

Feed your dog once or at most twice per day, wait 15 minutes, then pick up whatever is left over and put it away. Do this six days per week, and on the seventh day, give your dog only water. Young puppies, miniature or toy breeds, and dogs with certain illnesses should not be fasted for more than half a day (ask your veterinarian), but most dogs respond very well to this feeding cycle. They become more alert, attentive, and energetic – and no, it isn't because they are starving. Removing food between meals and fasting one day a week gives their digestive organs a well-deserved rest and sharpens the body's response to food.

Start by adding new food to old, maintaining the familiar taste and texture for as long as necessary. For young, active chow hounds in good health, combine 75 percent old food with 25 percent new food for a few days or a week, then feed half and half for a few days, and gradually reduce the old food to 25 percent or less, until the dog is eating all raw food.

For older dogs, go more slowly. If your dog walks away from unfamiliar foods, hide a fraction of a teaspoon of raw meat in the middle of his dinner. After several days, add more. If your dog has a favorite treat, add it, too. One dog I know refused to taste raw meat changed his mind when his owner mixed it with his all-time favorite food, asparagus!

Most of the dogs whose owners surveyed made the change within a month or two, but some took as long as a year. If you have any question about your dog's health before or during the transition, consult a holistic veterinarian or a breeder who has raised generations of your breed on an all-raw diet.

# Introducing Raw Meaty Bones

Most of the breeders and owners who feed a bone-based natural diet use whatever meaty bones are available at reasonable cost, such as lamb neck bones, chicken backs, and beef oxtails. To introduce a dog to raw bones, however, most experienced "raw feeders" use chicken wings or poultry necks.

"I recommend gradually switching dogs from cooked to raw foods and smashing or grinding raw bones until the dog is eating a completely raw diet, without any grains, yeast, milk, or dairy products," says Schultze. "If the dog has had digestive problems or has been on pharmaceutical drugs, especially antibiotics, within the past year, I would make the switch with the aid of digestive enzymes and non-dairy probiotics." Probiotics are beneficial bacteria such as acidophilus. Start with a fraction of the amount recommended on the label, gradually increasing to the recommended dosage.

Depending on its metabolism and activity level, a dog may need more or less, but two percent of its weight in raw meat and bones is

*This dog is enjoying a little dental exercise while trying to get the marrow out of this fresh bone. But chewing this sort of long, hard, and meatless bone fails to provide vital nutrients to the dog, and may even cause an aggressive chewer to crack or break a tooth. When feeding bones as part of an all-raw natural diet, most "raw feeders" rely heavily on raw chicken wings and necks as the primary, balanced source of minerals.*

a safe ballpark figure for a dog's total ration of food (one pound for a 50-pound dog). To provide the stomach exercise that helps prevent bloating, meat should be whole or in large chunks, not minced or ground. De Bairacli Levy recommends that bones be fed last, after the raw meat and vegetables, so that they are cushioned in the stomach.

Dogs new to bones often experience temporary diarrhea, constipation, or both as their systems adjust, especially if they eat large quantities. Remember to feed small amounts at first, start with bones that are easy to chew, smash them with a hammer to help your dog digest them, feed them last, and give adult dogs a digestive enzyme during the transition to raw food.

Chicken wings and necks are perfect "first bones" for teething puppies. Ann Mandelbaum, who breeds Standard Poodles in Connecticut, introduced a recent litter of pups to raw chicken wings when they were four weeks old. "Every day I gave one wing to each pair of puppies and let them work on it together," she says. "At first they gnawed most of the meat off and left the bones. By the middle of the week, they were nibbling on the ends, and by the end of the week, the bones were disappearing."

## Sample Daily Diet for a 50-lb. Dog

*In her book,* The Ultimate Diet: Natural Nutrition for Dogs and Cats, *Kymythy Schultze offers recipes and shopping lists for "raw feeders." Below is a sample recipe. Shultze, who breeds Newfoundlands and feeds all her dogs this diet, suggests taking a relaxed approach to the exact amounts of the ingredients, as long as you maintain the proportion of each type of ingredient to the next.*

*1) Raw meat: 3/4-1 cup muscle meat (plus occasional organ meat or egg)*

*2) Raw bone: 1 turkey neck or 6 chicken necks*

*3) Raw vegetables: 3 tablespoons pulped or grated vegetables*

*4) Supplements: 2 teaspoons kelp/alfalfa, 1 teaspoon cod-liver oil, 2 teaspoons flaxseed or fish body oil, 3,000-6,000 mg. vitamin C.*

In addition to their nutritional benefits, raw bones provide dental floss in the form of gristle and tendons. "You can always tell a bone-chewing dog," says holistic veterinarian Beverly Cappel, of Chestnut Ridge, New York. "They have the whitest, strongest, cleanest teeth."

Even when they appreciate the benefits of feeding raw bones, some owners are reluctant to provide them due to messiness (feed them outside!), because they have been frightened by veterinarians or another authority figure, or because they feel overwhelmed by the logistics of changing to a raw diet. Unfortunately, not including raw bones in a mostly-meat diet may create nutritional imbalances that cause serious harm. Billinghurst warns against the use of substitutes such as heat-sterilized bone meal and calcium supplements, for they can disrupt the natural balance of minerals in growing bodies and can cause, rather than prevent, hip dysplasia and other structural problems. There are over a hundred important elements in raw bones, bone marrow and connective tissue, all of which are vital to the health of joint cartilage, intervertebral discs, vascular walls and other parts of the canine body.

Raw bones that are soft enough for your pet to bite through, swallow and digest contain all of these nutrients. A small number of commercial supplements made from cold-sterilized raw bones contain most of them. If you are reluctant to feed your dog raw bones but want their nourishment, you can substitute either company's products or you can grind raw meaty bones in a meat grinder, keeping in mind that supplements and freshly ground bones cannot provide the tooth-cleaning benefits, hours of chewing pleasure, or stomach exercise that raw meaty bones provide.

# What about Bacteria?

Healthy dogs in the wild can eat just about any raw meat and survive, if not thrive. However, dogs on commercial food may not produce all the hydrochloric acid and beneficial bacteria they need for protection from pathogens.

If you are concerned about bacteria, you can disinfect large pieces of raw meat, raw bones, or eggs in the shell, soak them in a solution of 1/2 teaspoon original formula Clorox bleach per gallon water, several drops of 35-percent food-grade hydrogen peroxide in a sink of cold water (enough to create small bubbles but not enough to change the meat's color), OR 1/2 teaspoon liquid grapefruit seed extract in a sink of cold water. Let stand 5 to 10 minutes, rinse by soaking in plain water, and drain.

However, most raw feeders discontinue these disinfection practices as they gain confidence in their healthy dogs' ability to handle any bacteria that may be present in their raw food.

Most of the breeders and owners interviewed say their dog's raw meals are surprisingly easy to prepare. Some buy their meat at the supermarket while others arrange bulk shipments of organically grown meat and bones through holistic veterinarians, co-ops, dog clubs, and local hunters. For convenience, some manufacturers prepare raw food for dogs and freeze it for shipping.

"People are unnecessarily intimidated by raw-food diets," says pet nutritionist Pat McKay, author of *Reigning Cats and Dogs*. "That's unfortunate because it isn't difficult or time-consuming. In fact, if you spend more than 10 minutes a day feeding your dog, you either love to be in the kitchen or you're doing something wrong."

# Grains in a "Natural Diet"

While predators consume whatever grain is in their prey's digestive organs, wild herbivores have such limited access to seeds that a prey animal's stomach offers little or no grain. In addition, whatever grain the predator consumed has been at least partly digested, offering nutritional benefits that cooking cannot duplicate.

As Billinghurst notes, only sprouted grain, which is a live, raw food, is appropriate for dogs. To sprout grain, soak it overnight, drain, and leave it in an open glass jar at room temperature. Sprouted wheat, rye, barley, sunflower seeds, buckwheat, and other grains and seeds can be pureed and added to food or planted in trays for harvest a week later. Finely minced wheat grass and mature green sprouts are rich in enzymes, vitamins, and other nutrients.

To make vegetables more digestible, they can be pureed, ground, juiced, minced, pulverized, or fermented in the same process used to create sauerkraut. Sprinkle thinly sliced or grated vegetables with unrefined sea salt, then press them in a Japanese salad press or place them in a glass or ceramic bowl with a weight on top, such as a jar of water on a heavy plate. Lactic acid fermentation predigests the vegetables and releases their juice, imparting an aromatic, piquant flavor.

Cucumbers are ready to eat within a few hours, while shredded cabbage and root vegetables take a day or two. Pressed vegetables are taken seriously in Europe and Japan as digestive aids (lactic acid feeds beneficial bacteria) and as a cancer-prevention strategy. Refrigerated, they keep for weeks.

When pureed with sprouting grain and wheat grass, pressed vegetables resemble the partly digested contents of a prey animal's stomach. Their easily assimilated vitamins, minerals, enzymes, and other nutrients help dogs adjust to raw meat. Start with a small amount and gradually increase to about one tablespoon per 15 pounds of body weight per day, which, although much less than most books recommend for a dog's vegetable serving, is in keeping with a prey animal's proportions. Animal health instructor Kymythy Schultze describes how to use prey animals as a model for menu planning in her book, *The Ultimate Diet: Natural Nutrition for Dogs and Cats.*

For each 25 pounds of the dog's body weight, add to the vegetables 1/4 to 1/2 teaspoon cod liver oil, one teaspoon flaxseed or fish body oil, 1/2 teaspoon each powdered kelp, ginger, alfalfa, and milk thistle seed or other herbs, plus a food-source vitamin C supplement.

In addition, dogs making the transition to raw food are helped by Willard Water (a "catalyst-altered" water that reportedly improves the assimilation of nutrients and helps prevent symptoms of too-rapid detoxification), aloe vera juice or gel, and green foods such as spirulina or chlorella. Adjust a human product's label directions for your dog's weight by assuming that the human weighs 120 to 150 pounds.

THERE ARE OVER A HUNDRED IMPORTANT

ELEMENTS IN RAW BONES, BONE MARROW

AND CONNECTIVE TISSUE, ALL OF WHICH

ARE VITAL TO THE HEALTH OF JOINT

CARTILAGE, INTERVERTEBRAL DISCS,

VASCULAR WALLS AND OTHER PARTS OF

THE CANINE BODY.

# Switching Slowly But Surely

Most dogs make the transition to a raw diet without complications, but there are always exceptions. We've heard of individual dogs who have required medical attention following a dramatic diet change.

Hemorrhagic gastroenteritis is often blamed on a too-rapid change of diet, and a dog or puppy that is not equipped to deal with raw bones may find its system overwhelmed if they are suddenly provided.

When her mother's 10-year-old Labrador Retriever came to live with New York trainer Nancy Strouss, she had been eating a supermarket kibble all her life. Strouss offered the Lab everything she fed her Goldens, and within a week, Samantha's coat was shining, her eyes were brighter, and her gait improved. But then she started throwing up.

"There was no pattern to it," says Strouss. "Sometimes it was bile and sometimes undigested food; sometimes she vomited right after dinner and sometimes in the middle of the night or first thing in the morning. Because my Goldens stayed healthy, I knew there was nothing wrong with the food, and she still looked great and had lots of energy, so I hoped this symptom would pass as she adjusted." The vomiting stopped after seven days, but it was replaced by something worse: a week of uncontrollable diarrhea.

Samantha was experiencing the symptoms of too-rapid detoxification, which can happen when the diet is drastically changed. To help Samantha recover, Strouss drastically reduced the raw protein and for two weeks fed her cooked potatoes, rice, leeks, and boiled chicken with liver-supporting supplements.

Samantha responded immediately. Gradually over the next two weeks, Strouss replaced the cooked chicken with raw meat and the cooked potatoes with raw vegetables.

Today, four months after her arrival, Samantha eats all raw food, including meaty bones, and has no digestive problems. "She's almost 11, but she acts like a two-year-old," says Strouss. "She runs, jumps, and plays ball, her coat continues to improve, her eyes are clear, she has no ear infections, her arthritis has disappeared, and she never steals food, which she did on a daily basis in her old home." ❧

# 10

# Fruits & Vegetables: Good For Your Dog

*Low calorie snack or important ingredients in your pet's balanced diet? Here's what we think.*

We are a nation of snackers as well as pet lovers. Is it any wonder that we've transferred our own fondness for eating between meals to our dogs? We justify treats as rewards for good behavior, we give our dogs a biscuit when we're having a snack ourselves, and often give in to our dog's pleading expression for a doggy snack.

The treats we eat and those we feed to our dogs are the source of weight problems for both our species. Chips, cookies, and ice cream pack on the pounds in humans; so do dog biscuits in our canine friends. This is why nutritionists give a qualified nod to giving fruits and vegetables to our dogs instead of biscuits if we're intent on dispensing treats.

"It's best not to get into the habit of feeding your dog treats, but if food already is an important part of your relationship, vegetables are a lower-calorie substitute for dog biscuits," says Dr. Rebecca Remillard, nutritionist at Angell Memorial Hospital in Boston and for the Massachusetts Society for the Prevention of Cruelty to Animals (MSPCA).

"If you have to give a treat, try substituting fruit such as grapes, pieces of apple, or melon," she notes. "Dogs can't digest most of it, and fruits add fiber to their diet. I wish more people would feed vegetables or fruit as treats instead of feeding their dogs snack food."

Just as we justify our own snacking, dog owners may think that treats, even healthy snacks like fruit and vegetables, are giving dogs nutrients they need. "What about the extra vitamin C my dog is getting from the fruit I give him?" you may ask. The short answer is, dogs don't really need it. Although Vitamin C is essential for humans, current veterinary research indicates that dogs don1t benefit from supplemental amounts of Vitamin C; their own bodies synthesize what they need, according to animal nutritionists.

At Ralston Purina, Dottie LaFlamme, DVM., research fellow, and nutritionist notes, "Most nutritionists would say that dogs don't need fruits and vegetables."

---

CURRENT VETERINARY RESEARCH INDICATES THAT DOGS DON'T BENEFIT FROM SUPPLEMENTAL AMOUNTS OF VITAMIN C; THEIR OWN BODIES SYNTHESIZE WHAT THEY NEED, ACCORDING TO ANIMAL NUTRITIONISTS.

---

Unlike humans, dogs don't need to get their nutrients from eating according to the food pyramid, balancing proteins with carbohydrates and fats, Dr. LaFlamme says. "If a dog is being fed a high quality commercial pet food, he's getting all the nutrients he needs."

Having said that, nutritionists also recognize that most dog owners love to give their pets treats. The numbers of overweight dogs (some studies suggest that up to 30% of dogs seen by veterinarians are overweight) is a testament to our misplaced devotion.

The benefit, then, to giving fruit or vegetables as treats is their low-calorie content. This is especially true for a dog who's being treated for obesity with a restricted diet, and who is having a hard time dealing with lesser quantities of food.

LaFlamme recommends diluting the number of calories an overweight dog is consuming by adding a can of vegetables to his food. "This helps the dog to feel he's getting more to eat," she explains, "and it makes the food more palatable for the dog."

Fruits or vegetables can also be a useful part of behavior training.

For a dog who's upset at being left alone, stalks of celery stuffed with peanut butter can be a tasty treat that helps ease the pangs of separation. Dogs also like the crunch!

Within the snack alternatives represented by fruits and vegetables, nutritionists point out a few you might want to avoid. **Stay away from onions and garlic.** Dr. Remillard notes that they contain an alkaloid compound that can damage red blood cells. Onions seem to be the main offender here, while some owners, including veterinarians, permit their dogs garlic-flavored treats. And an overabundance of fibrous vegetables like Brussels sprouts and kale can cause flatulence.

Just as you'd wash any fruit or vegetable you'd eat, do the same when you feed them to your dog. "Raw fruits and vegetables can have bacterial microbes; washing them before eating is just as important for dogs as it is for humans," Dr. Remillard says.

# What Dogs Like

There's quite a variety among fruits and vegetables dog owners feed to their pets. Carrots and apples were among the most common raw fruits and vegetables, while a surprising number of broccoli fans are cooking and serving florets to their dogs with good response. "Our dogs love broccoli and even the green water in which the broccoli has been cooked," reported one owner.

Labradors and golden retrievers seem to be the most omnivorous. From owners of these breeds there are reports of their dogs eating bananas, raisins, tomatoes, even wild berries right off the bushes. One golden retriever eats orange sections as a nightly snack. "She won't go to sleep until she has her oranges," her owner says.

# Alternative Views

While mainstream nutritionists minimize the importance of fruit and vegetables to a well balanced diet for normal-weight dogs, a committed minority follow an all-natural approach, including them in addition to or in place of raw and cooked meats.

Celeste Yarnall is an outspoken pet author from Beverly Hills, California who recommends raw and cooked vegetables and fruit as part of a diet based on raw meat. (Most nutritionists, including those at Tufts, caution strongly that raw meat can be dangerous because of the possibility of contamination by salmonella or other organisms.)

Yarnall promotes an all-natural diet, supplemented with vitamins, minerals, and fatty acids, in her book, *Natural Dog Care*, and web site (celestialpets.com). "I'm about balanced diets for dogs," Yarnall said in an interview. For normal dogs, she recommends a diet consisting of one-third raw meat, and two-thirds vegetables—broccoli, zucchini, carrots, and fruits and grains.

Yarnall, agrees she's considered a radical by most pet nutritionists, and also feeds her 12-year-old collie, Connie, leftovers from her own meals. "She loves salmon and steaks, and when I bake a potato for myself, I always bake an extra for Connie."

Other holistic practitioners suggest that a diet that includes vegetables and grains (even ground pumpkin seeds) may help prevent worms from taking up residence in a dog's intestinal tract—or help alleviate the condition. While the occasional raw carrot or apple makes a good treat, you can try steaming or pureeing vegetables and fruits to blend in with a dog's regular food.

When choosing a dietary supplement or substitutes for your dog, even an innocuous-sounding one like fruit or vegetables, it's best to check first with your veterinarian. This is especially true if you plan on making changes that include a greater share of "people" food.

# Why Vegetables?

"Feeding your dog fresh, whole foods is vital for overall health," says Dr. Christina Chambreau, a well-known holistic veterinarian with a practice near Baltimore, Maryland. Fresh, raw meat should provide the majority of a dog's diet, Chambreau says, feeding the least-processed – and preferably organic – foods does more to support health than almost any other dog-care practice. That's because nutrients are in their most bio-available state when they are fresh and uncooked.

Supplementing "dead," cooked foods with synthetic vitamins and minerals simply isn't nearly as beneficial as feeding whole food sources. One reason is that synthetic vitamins interact differently with minerals in the body.

For example, man-made ascorbic acid can deplete copper levels, but the vitamin C from food sources does not. And in some cases, synthetic vitamins are stereo-isomers (mirror images) of natural vitamins, but can't bind to receptor sites in the body the same way as natural vitamins.

Vegetables offer other benefits. They are relatively inexpensive (compared to meats, fruits, and whole grains. They are also digested relatively well, especially compared to grains. The high carbohydrates provided by grains provide a substrate for bacterial over-growth, with the resultant production of toxic metabolites that cause a variety of digestive problems such as gas and diarrhea.

Vegetables are also much lower in sugar than fruits; too much sugar in a dog's diet can overstimulate the production of stomach acids. And some dog owners find vegetables to be a convenient, nutritious, but lower-calorie replacement for kibble in a dieting dog's food bowl. (Fills 'em up without plumping 'em up!)

# Vegetables and Their Nutrients

■ *Vitamin A: Essential for vision, especially night vision, immune system health, maintenance of soft mucous tissues and normal growth. Carrots, collard greens, beet greens, cress, mustard greens, broccoli, red peppers, winter squash, yams, and sweet potatoes.*

■ *Vitamin B Complex: Vital to the health of the nervous system. These are the most fragile and heat sensitive vitamins. Beans, peas, dark green leafy vegetables.*

■ *Vitamin C: A powerful antioxidant important to repairing tissues and immune system health, vital to improve collagen and helps prevent arthritis and joint problems. Tomatoes, sweet potatoes, red and green peppers.*

■ *Vitamin E: An antioxidant which speeds the healing of wounds and burns, improves the assimilation and distribution of nutrients in the body, keeps the heart healthy, invigorates older animals, slows the symptoms of aging, improves the skin and coat of all animals, and boosts resistance to disease. High levels yield stronger, healthier litters. Vegetable oils, dark green, leafy vegetables, avocados.*

■ *Vitamin K: A blood clotting regulator, vitamin K is essential for kidney function and bone metabolism. Cabbage, turnip greens, and other dark leafy greens.*

■ *Minerals: Assist the body with vitamin absorption, digestion, and the health of every body system –circulatory, cardiac, reproductive system, skin, skeletal, vascular, and all else. All vegetables contain some minerals.*

# Preparation Is Important

Because dogs have short intestinal tracts, they do need a little help to efficiently break down plant cell walls and extract the nutrients. This can be accomplished without much effort, and the payoff in natural vitamin supplementation is well worth it for your pet in terms of prevention of disease and overall health.

Dr. Pat Bradley, a holistic veterinarian with a practice in Conway, Arkansas, explains. "Each raw fruit and vegetable contains the enzymes necessary to break it down within its cells. That's what you're seeing when you drop an apple; the bruising is a release of enzymes. Feeding raw foods is a good idea because all the enzymes necessary to break down that particular food are there. However, because a dog's digestive system is so short, the digestive process is quick. Feeding raw foods, with the enzymes still present, can speed the process of digestion, increasing nutrient availability with less stress on the system."

Some people use vegetables such as carrots as snacks to alleviate doggie boredom and for chewing exercise. But in order to help your dog digest plant material, without it passing right through them undigested, you should puree, finely grind, or grate the vegetables. Some dog owners put the vegetables through a blender or food processor to break them down to a smooth consistency.

Any or all of the following vegetables can be used alone or in combination: broccoli, Brussels sprouts, cabbage, carrots, cauliflower, celery, corn, green beans, greens, kohlrabi, okra, parsnips, peas, pumpkin, sprouts, squash, sweet potatoes, turnips, and rutabagas.

While the enzymes, vitamins, and antioxidants present in foods are diminished by cooking, it may be beneficial to lightly steam some types of vegetables to assist the breakdown of cell walls. Some of the vegetables that are more palatable and digestible when slightly cooked include potatoes, rutabagas, and asparagus. As stated earlier, avoid onions and garlic.

Veterinarians say your dog may consume up to one third of his total meal by volume in veggies, but watch your dog. Introduce all new foods slowly over time to help your pet adjust to changes in her diet. Notice what she eats first and what she leaves in her dish. Notice too, what passes undigested in her stools; could there be another way to prepare that food to increase digestibility? Evaluate the dog for energy levels, haircoat, overall health and then evaluate her again after feeding vegetables for a month. Reduce or increase the amount of vegetables accordingly. ❧

# 11

# The Meat of the Matter

*Commercial dog food was invented in 1860.*
*Until then, the ancestral diet of dogs*
*was mostly raw meat.*

D og food as we know it today—either crumbly bits of kibble packaged in bags and boxes or gloopy meat-based concoctions sealed into cans—was invented in 1860. Think about that for a moment: Our great-grandparents and great-great-grandparents raised dogs completely without the benefit of Purina. Before 1860, no one poured a pile of chow from a bag marked, "Dog." But everyone who had a dog knew what dogs liked to eat and how to feed them.a

Considering how many thousands of years that dogs have survived while living in our homes and sharing our meals, it is interesting that most dog owners are shocked and perplexed when it is suggested that they might want to consider giving up their cans and bags of dog food.

"Well then, what WOULD I feed my dog?!" they say.

The answer is food...real food...raw food, the kind of food that canines have been living and thriving on for the last few centuries! Yes, we are talking (mostly) about meat.

In the last few years, nutrition experts have "rediscovered" the value of a paleolithic diet for humans—one that includes far more fruits and vegetables and far fewer grains than we eat now, a certain amount of fresh meat, and certainly no dairy products.

Veterinary nutritionists and holistic veterinarians can likewise tell you about the many benefits of feeding your dog his ancestral diet. The actual recipes are speculative, of course, but there is no doubt about the major constituent of the diet: raw meat.

Duplicating this diet as closely as possible is said to have numerous benefits. Holistic veterinarians and breeders who use a raw-meat diet say it can make itching dogs stop scratching, thin, dull coats become thicker and shinier, and apathetic dogs regain enthusiasm for life. Females who have had difficulty conceiving or carrying puppies to term become pregnant and bear healthy puppies.

"Having raised animals on commercial pet food, and now, having raised animals on raw meat, there's no comparison," says Celeste Yarnall, a pet nutrition specialist and author of *Natural Cat Care*, and *Natural Dog Care*. "Animals who are fed an appropriate raw-meat diet are alive, they glow from whisker to tail tip. They are happy and comfortable in their skins."

# Why Is Raw Meat Better?

There are numerous reasons why dogs might do better on a diet largely comprised of meat. Foremost, says Yarnall, is that dogs' bodies are designed to produce only about 25 percent of the enzymes they need to digest their food; the remaining 75 percent should be within the food they eat.

All raw foods contain the enzymes the body needs to digest the food. But when you cook foods, the enzymes are destroyed. In order to digest a food devoid of enzymes, the body needs to work overtime to produce its own digestive enzymes to break down the food. Cooking also destroys a large percentage of the food's nutrients. Some foods lose as much as half of their vitamins when they are cooked.

"It is far more dangerous to feed a dog commercial dog foods than it is to feed him raw meat," says Celeste Yarnall.

Many holistic veterinarians believe the resulting wear and tear on the pancreas may be responsible, in turn, for other health problems. In her book, *The Natural Dog*, Mary Brennan, DVM, says that many research studies have linked enzyme deficiencies and diseases, both acute and chronic. To counter this, one can supplement the dog with digestive enzymes, or feed raw food!

And, finally, to some degree cooking generates a certain amount of toxins in food. Raw food enthusiasts cite the fact that the number of white blood cells circulating in the bloodstream usually doubles or triples immediately following consumption of a cooked food meal.But the number does not rise when raw food is eaten. A body that initiates such an "attacking" immune response to every cooked meal wastes much of its precious resources sidetracked in a needless battle.

# Overcoming Objections

It is testimony to our skeptical times that most people who feed their dogs raw food spend more of their time defending their decision than describing the benefits of their diets. Fortunately the experts are ready with answers to typical questions:

■ **What about the danger of bacteria and food poisoning?**

Many people fear bacterial contamination and resultant food poisoning so much that they cannot entertain the idea of feeding their dog raw meat. To these people, Yarnall says, "So many dogs live with sub-clinical medical conditions all their lives, dying of cancer, kidney failure, liver disease, arthritis, and every other combination of the diseases . . . I'd rather take my chances against the bacteria, and feed the food that best supports dogs' health."

This is not to say that Yarnall and other raw feeders disregard the threat of contamination. Most use some method to disinfect the meat they feed their dogs and observe "safe-meat" handling techniques .

"Of course you have to practice safe hygiene. You have to be more intelligent than someone who uses a can opener to prepare their dogs' meal. But the benefits outweigh the risks by so much," says Yarnall.

■ **Doesn't this cost a lot?**

There's no doubt about it: feeding meat on a regular basis costs more than feeding dog food. But according to the experts, the improvement in the dog's health will more than offset the price of the diet.

Yarnall says she could prove this one on a graph. "I don't spend money having my veterinarian treat my dog for flea problems and allergies and fungus problems and heartworm and all the other diseases brought on by poor nutrition," she says. "I spend my money on the food, instead."

Dr. Brennan tells of a client who raised Yorkshire Terriers and Lhasa apso, and was concerned about the increased cost of feeding a higher quality diet. However, at Brennan's urging, she tried the diet, and in the next heat cycle, she saw a 75 percent improvement in her dogs' conception rate, proving that the change was cost-effective to her business.

We should add that the above question made one raw feeder we spoke get angry. "So, if I want to save money I should raise my children on Top Ramen and generic Cheerios?" she exploded. "I tell people that if you can't afford to feed three children properly, you shouldn't have three children, and they understand me. But when I say that if you can't afford to feed three dogs properly, you shouldn't have three dogs, they come unglued. Why people will try to defend being cheap with the health and well-being of their loved ones is beyond me."

■ **Isn't dealing with meat inconvenient?**

Fortunately, the market takes care of all inconveniences. There are a number of companies springing up to cater to those who don't want to take the time to select, buy, and prepare meat for their dogs Others buy enough meat for a week or two or even a month, and spend a couple of hours on that day preparing and separating the food into individual portions that they then freeze. Then, each night they transfer the next day's meal into the refrigerator, where it can thaw safely for feeding the next day.

■ **Why would my veterinarian tell me to feed Brand X, if it is so bad for my dog?**

We'll let Celeste Yarnall answer this one:

"If you feed your dog nothing but commercial pet foods, you will have a very happy veterinarian, because your dog will be a patient for life. Go on into the veterinarian's office and get your bags and your cans, and you will come back with a dog who has cancer, with dripping orifices, with skin problems and allergies, and worse. Veterinarians are wonderful people, don't get me wrong, but they have been educated very poorly in nutrition.

"Guess where most veterinarians got their education? Who donates the largest amounts of money to university vet schools? Guess who writes the textbooks? The pharmaceutical industry and the pet food companies, that's who! So is it any wonder that the veterinarians are all taught that dogs are better off eating food from a bag or a can?"

■ **I can see this diet working for wolves, but our modern dogs are vastly different animals . . . aren't they?**

Actually, the wolf and the dog are not that far apart. It's true that we have bred them to look very different from their wolf ancestors, but what's "under the hood" is still essentially the same. Dogs have been living with us for a long time, but they still have 42 shredding teeth; they haven't suddenly grown big grinding teeth like ours!

# How To Feed Meat

OK, let's assume you are sold on a raw meat diet. Next question: How do you go about formulating a raw-meat diet? Recipes for home-made dog food abound, and every book on our resource list includes at least one. But despite numerous small variations of opinion regarding supplements, the basic proportions of raw meat to grains to vegetable matter is roughly the same.

Yarnall suggests formulating a diet that is comprised of about 40 percent meat, and 30 percent vegetables, and 30 percent grains. She uses about 60 percent muscle meat and about 40 percent of organ meat (kidneys, liver, or heart). The vegetables vary, and are prepared, raw, in a food processor. Yarnall uses only slow cooked oatmeal (the 30-minute type) or barley flakes. She adds enough purified water to make the mixture the consistency of a thick chili. Yarnall supplements this food with an essential fatty acid supplement and a small amount of bone meal. For comparison, McKinnon uses a diet comprised of about 30-40 percent meat, fish, or eggs, 40-50 percent grains, and 20 percent vegetables.

Some raw feeders eschew the use of grains altogether, since grains are not technically part of the dog's ancestral diet. Dr. Russell Swift, a Florida veterinarian who has had a long-time interest in pet nutrition, was among the first to question the need for grains in dog food. His recipe for home-made dog food contains a smaller amount of grain than many authorities. He suggests using just 1/4 cup of oats or multi-grain hot cereal and 1/4 to 1/2 cup of chopped raw vegetables to every 1/2 pound (about a cup) of raw meat.

Most raw food enthusiasts size the dog's meals at about two to three percent of the dog's body weight daily. (A 50-pound dog would get 1 to 1 1/2 pounds of food a day.) Watch your dog's weight and condition and adjust the amount accordingly—reduce the amount if he starts gaining weight, increase the amount if he begins to get too slim.

That last advice may sound unscientific, but it's not. It's representative of the kind of thinking—the whole mindset—that you should bring to the task of feeding meat to your dog. It's simple. It's intuitive. It's natural. It's how dogs are supposed to eat. ❧

# 12

# The Fuss Over Fiber

*Does dietary fiber—the nondigestible component
of fruits, vegetables, seeds, and grains—
play a significant role in the canine diet?*

Dietary fiber has received considerable attention for its crucial role in the human diet. Now, nutritionists are studying—and debating—fiber's significance in the canine diet. Experts recommend that people eat lots of fiber because it reduces the risk of colon cancer and helps prevent high blood pressure and coronary artery disease. However, these three diseases are rare in dogs, and it's unclear whether fiber is physiologically essential for dogs in the same way that protein, fat, vitamins, minerals, and water are.

"Whether dogs need fiber at all is controversial," says Dr. Lisa Freeman, assistant professor and nutritionist at Tufts University School of Veterinary Medicine. "There is no officially established minimum fiber requirement for dogs." Still, many people feel fiber is important to canine health.

## Form and Function

Fiber resists the chemical breakdown action of Fido's digestive enzymes, but it does absorb water and swell. Some types of fiber help move food through the digestive system faster, while others slow down the transit time. Fiber also distends a dog's large intestine and thus stimulates defecation.

The main sources of dietary fiber are cellulose and hemicellulose (found in plant cell walls), pectin (found in fruits), gums (viscous substances exuded by plants that solidify when dried), and lignin (the "cement" that holds plant cell walls together). Nutritionists categorize these fiber sources according to how completely they dissolve in water (solubility) and the degree to which intestinal bacteria break them down into fatty acids (fermentability).

Soluble fiber (pectin, gums, and some forms of hemicellulose such as psyllium) attracts water, helps soften stools, and is usually more fermentable than insoluble fiber (cellulose, lignin, and some forms of hemicellulose such as wheat bran). Although a dog cannot use the resulting fatty acids from fermented fiber as an energy source, some nutritionists believe these acids may contribute to the health of the large intestine. But for dogs, the real role, if any, of fiber solubility and fermentability is a "hot potato" topic among veterinary nutritionists.

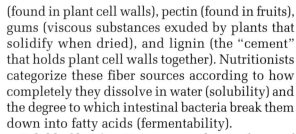

## Disease-Management Debate

The digestive characteristics of fiber give it potential health benefits, but there's disagreement as to what those benefits are. For example, some dog-food manufacturers add extra fiber—particularly insoluble fiber—to weight-loss diets because some studies suggest it makes a dog feel full. However, other studies have concluded that fiber does not impart a full feeling, so not all food manufacturers add extra fiber to their calorie-restricted formulas.

Fiber can sometimes help manage diabetes mellitus, the high-blood-sugar condition that results from deficiency of the hormone insulin. Fiber , slows intestinal absorption of glucose, thereby helping control blood-sugar levels. Similarly, veterinarians have used high-fiber diets to help manage some cases of inflammatory bowel disease (a group of chronic gastrointestinal disorders), even though high fiber exacerbates the condition in other cases. Lots of fiber is not indicated, however, for diabetic dogs that have trouble keeping on weight because such diets tend to be low in calories.

# Fiber's Faults

There are potential downsides to fiber-filled dog diets. Fiber typically increases a dog's stool volume, which may pose clean-up problems for some owners. Studies have also suggested that diets high in insoluble fiber may inhibit digestive absorption of some important minerals. Therefore, manufacturers need to carefully maintain adequate nutrient proportions in high-fiber dog food to compensate for potential absorption reductions.

Unfortunately, reading dog-food labels won't help clarify the fiber controversy much. That's because the actual dietary-fiber content in dog food can be as much as two to five times higher than the content listed as crude fiber (the residue after laboratories chemically "digest" food) in the label's guaranteed analysis. Hence, making brand-to-brand comparisons is difficult.

When it comes to fiber in dog food, the only indisputable fact is that different foods contain different levels and types of fiber. One other thing is clear: "Every dog has its individual nutrient requirements," emphasizes Dr. Freeman. "So it's important to talk to your veterinarian to determine the best level and type of fiber for your dog." If you and your veterinarian decide to go the high-fiber route, introduce your dog to the new diet gradually and closely monitor its response to the dietary change. ❧

# 13

# Tops in Treats

*The good news: There are more good
—even GREAT—
treats on the market than ever.*

Though the "rising tide of health awareness" doesn't seem to have raised the consciousness of the titanic mainstream dog food industry much, we've found some things we like in the area of dog treats.

If you're using treats for training purposes, we recommend that you find one with the highest meat content available. Grain products coated in oils can be attractive to dogs, but to provide an irresistible incentive to perform whatever feats of canine agility or obedience you desire, the dog's gotta know: "Where's the beef?"

Our general suggestions are to stay away from "big-name" commercial treats found in grocery stores, look for products that meet our selection criteria, and let your dog's health and appetite be your best guide.

## Ingredients We Want To See

■ We like meat-based treats for dogs. Most commercial dog treats are grain-based, but treats with meat in them more closely simulate a dog's natural diet.

■ Top-quality, whole ingredients like oatmeal, rice, wheat, vegetables, fruits, nuts, and eggs.

■ We want to see foods that are kept fresh with natural preservatives like vitamin C and E (often listed as "mixed-tocopherols").

■ We award bonus points for organic foods.

■ Natural, food-based sweeteners, such as applesauce, molasses, or honey. When choosing a dog food, something the dog will eat every day of his life, we generally disapprove of the use of sweeteners. However, with treats, we're more relaxed about our usual restriction on sugars, which make the snack more palatable. Do avoid artificial or lower-quality substances such as corn syrup, sucrose, and ammoniated glycyrrhizin.

Also, be aware that flavor enhancers such as salt and sugar are sometimes used to make poor-quality ingredients tastier. If the product contains "good stuff," your dog will want it.

# Top Picks

■ **Pro-Treat's Freeze Dried Beef Liver**: This treat contains only one ingredient—raw beef liver that has been freeze-dried so it doesn't requires any preservatives or additives. Many professional dog trainers use dried liver for rewarding their canine pupils, since dogs seem to be able to smell the rich food at 100 paces and relish the taste, increasing their motivation to perform well. One caution: this is an extremely rich food, containing at least 50% protein. It's also high in vitamin A, which is one nutrient that dogs can get too much of. Feed it in small amounts only, no matter how adorable your dog can be after he sees the bag.

■ **Old Mother Hubbard's Natural Liv'r' Crunch**: Wheat flour, cane molasses, liver, poultry meal, dried beet pulp, animal fat preserved with mixed tocopherols, caramel, cultured whey, brewers rice, wheat germ meal. Because of the high liver content, the same warning above goes for these little biscuits, too; go easy.

■ **Nancy Anne's Pampered Pet Treats**: Honey & Oatmeal treats contain rolled oats, partially hydrogenated soybean oil, honey, rice flour, soy flour, water, dried whey, whole dried eggs, oat bran (only nine ingredients). Since these treats contain no meat at all, they are a valuable alternative for dogs with allergies to animal fats and meat. The high amount of oil and honey seems to make up for the lack of meat to attract dogs' appetites.

■ **California Natural Health Bar**: Lamb meal, whole ground rice, oatmeal, flaxseed meal, sunflower oil (preserved with vitamin E, vitamins and minerals). We're fans of the California Natural dog food, and, happily, the makers have only slightly altered the simple, elegant formula of the food to make these treats. Note that this is a wheat- and corn-free treat. We've got nothing against wheat and corn per se, but these ingredients are some of the more common food allergens. In order for a treat to be a real treat, of course, it must be, above all, extremely palatable. Lamb meal at the top of the list of ingredients seems to provide the necessary attractiveness; all the "test dogs" we offered them to took the treats quite readily.

■ **Doggie Divines** (Chicken Carrot): Organic stone-ground whole wheat flour, Rice Dream Organic Original (contains filtered water, organic brown rice, expeller pressed oleic safflower oil, sea salt), Eberly's organic chicken, organic carrots, rosemary, parsley, garlic.

■ **Brunzi's Best**: has made the most serious commitment to using organic foods that you will find in the pet food industry. Most, rather than just one or two, ingredients in Brunzi's treats are organic. And, rather than taking chances with municipal water, Brunzi's has used "Rice Dream," an organic brown rice beverage (made with filtered water) for moistening the dough. Even the meat sources are organic, a step higher in quality than "free-range."

The chicken/carrot flavor is Brunzi's only meat-based biscuit; while they also make a number of other flavors (of a similarly high quality), we've selected the chicken-based cookie for its superior palatability. The company also makes two wheat-and corn-free biscuits (peanut butter and oatmeal raisin cookies). Doggie Divines are available in a number of different-sized packages, including gift packs.

■ **Liver Biscotti**: USDA select beef liver (human grade), Giusto's organic whole wheat flour, Giusto's 20% bran flour, water, fresh carrots, eggs, garlic. Woolf Products' Liver Biscotti is perhaps the best treat for training that we've ever come across. The draw, of course, is the liver, which dogs love. But unlike feeding pure, freeze-dried liver, which contains so much vitamin A that you have to limit your dog's daily consumption, you don't have to worry about feeding too much Liver Biscotti, "cut" as it is with wheat, carrots, eggs, etc. Also, the treat is made in small cubes and chunks, most smaller than sugar cubes. Even though the pieces are small, they seemed to be highly sought-after by our test dogs; we noticed that we got a lot more compliance from our canine companions when there was Liver Biscotti to be handed out. This is a simple, healthy, and affordable treat.

■ **Liver Crisps**: Treats that contain meat simply appeal to more dogs than those without. Dancing Dog Bakery also features "mostly organic" treats, two of which contain meat (the Liver Crisp flavor uses beef liver, and the Hearty Beef and Grains uses beef). Each of Dancing Dog's six flavors is formulated simply, with wholesome, whole foods. Two ("Gingerbread Guys" and "Garden Biscuits") are made without wheat or corn. Most ingredients grown on the proprietor's own farm.

■ **Lick Your Chops "4 Cheese Dog Biscuits"**: The cheese flavor contains only whole grain stone ground wheat flour, corn meal, shortening, whole eggs, powdered milk, molasses, parmesan cheese, Monterey Jack cheese, cheddar cheese, garlic, wheat germ, parsley, and beef broth. Dogs with dairy intolerances will enjoy the Italian style biscuits, which are just as good.

■ **Nature's Animals All Natural Dog Biscuits**: Contain whole wheat flour, wheat bran, lamb, ground brown rice corn oil, parsley, garlic, baking soda, preserved with mixed tocopherols (a source of vitamin E). These biscuits have an attractive look and texture and a fresh grain smell to them.

■ **Precise's "Healthy Habit"**: Not quite as healthy as the products above. However, they are perhaps the most widely distributed of the products listed here, and leagues ahead of the typical "junk food" biscuits found in supermarkets and pet "superstores." They contain wheat flour, chicken, oat flour, ground rice, ground corn, wheat germ meal, animal fat preserved with lecithin, brewers yeast, and garlic.

# Very Good Treats

■ **Burt's Bones**: Whole wheat flour, corn meal, fresh parsley and garlic, whole eggs, chicken broth, vegetable oil. A perfectly fine treat, but not quite of the quality found in our "Top Picks." Burt's Bones contain nice, whole foods, and are attractively packaged for gift giving.

■ **Howlin' Gourmet**: Organically grown wheat flour, oat flour, unsalted roasted peanut butter, unsalted roasted peanuts, whole eggs, honey, canola oil. Dancing Paws, maker of top-quality supplements, has done a fine job of formulating its dog treats. Each contains at least one organic ingredient. Dancing Paws declines using meat in its products, using "vegetarian chicken stock" in its "Chicken Pot Pie," and "vegetarian bacon bits" in its "Smokehouse Favorite."

■ **Mr. Barky's Vegetarian Dog Biscuits**: Wheat flour, whole oat groats, whole ground brown rice, whole ground yellow corn, whole barley, soy flour, sunflower oil. Only whole grains are used in this perfectly healthy formula. However, we found Mr. Barky's to be attractive to only the most food-motivated test dogs; without something extra-yummy in them, the picky eaters turned these treats down.

■ **Poochie Pretzels**: Barley flour, non-fat powdered milk, bottled water, egg, honey, soybean oil, vegetable broth, spices. Poochie Pretzels is just one of Molly's many good-quality treats, including several wheat- and corn-free treats. Molly's uses whole foods, several organic ingredients, and "Veg-A-Fed" eggs.

# The Cookie Jar

*If buying your dog's cookies make you feel like a "bad parent," here's a recipe for baking them yourself.*

## Barney's Best Spirulina, Carob & Oat Biscuits

*1 cup whole wheat flour*
*1 cup oat flour (available in health food stores or blend oatmeal in a blender until consistency of flour)*
*1/4 cup carob\* powder (get at health food store)*
*1/2 cup raw wheat germ*
*1 teaspoon Spirulina (available in health food stores and pharmacies)*
*1 tablespoon molasses ( I use blackstrap molasses; it's loaded with nutrients)*
*3/4 cup vegetable broth*
*Cornmeal*
*Preheat the oven to 300 degrees.*

*1) In a bowl add the first five ingredients and combine .*
*2) In a smaller bowl, mix the molasses into the vegetable broth until well blended.*
*3) Add the flour mixture to the liquid, making a thick dough.*
*4) Form dough into a ball. Sprinkle cornmeal onto a clean, dry surface and roll dough out on the cornmeal. Roll to 1/4 of an inch thick. You should flip the dough over periodically to prevent sticking and to coat both sides with the cornmeal. Cut rolled dough into circles.*
*5) Grease cookie sheet, and arrange biscuits on the sheet. Prick each cookie with a fork.*
*6) Bake in the oven for 15-20 minutes.*
*7) Let cool in the oven overnight or on wire racks. Store in the refrigerator. "Bone" Appetit!*

*\*Carob is a chocolate substitute that is very nutritious and contains no theobromine, the.substance in chocolate that is toxic to dogs.*

# Ingredients We Don't Want To See

■ No artificial preservatives, such as BHA, BHT, potassium sorbate, sodium nitrate (used for dual purposes, preservative and coloring) and especially, ethoxyquin.
■ No artificial colors.
■ No products with the term "flavor" in the ingredients list (chicken flavor, liver flavor). This indicates the contents don't have enough of their own good flavor – not the mark of quality ingredients.
■ No propylene glycol, which is used to keep foods moist.
■ No food "fragments" or by-products. The dog food industry is a well-known dumping ground for waste products from the human food industry. A treat that contains "whole wheat" is infinitely healthier than one that has had wheat bran, wheat middlings, and wheat germ. Meat ingredients should be whole, too. This is indicated by the notation "Chicken," "lamb," "beef," etc., rather than "chicken by-products," or, worse, "poultry by-products," for instance. "Chicken meal" is better than "chicken by-products," but just plain "chicken" would be better. A product made with "organically raised chicken" would be best of all.

# Just Missed Our List

■ **Healthy Habit Dog Treats** (Lamb & Rice): Eliminated because contains low-quality "animal fat."
■ **Healthy Snacks Dog Biscuits**: Eliminated because the marketing and the ingredients don't add up. Contains food fragments (corn gluten meal) and unidentified "meat meal."
■ **Nutro Crunchers**: Eliminated because there are four forms of wheat, including fragments: wheat flour, whole wheat, wheat starch, wheat bran, and corn gluten meal.
■ **Power Bark**: Eliminated because of rice syrup (its second ingredient) and molasses (its fourth) plus salt (ninth); sweet and salty junk food.

# Not Recommended

If you have learned to recognize the healthy and the poor-quality ingredients on the labels of your dog's foods you'll see that products like the following don't have anything of value to offer your dog. Check out the top 10 ingredients in each of these popular brands of dog treats (consider that these are the top 10 ingredients only; there are many more chemicals in each):

■ **Nutro Training Bits:** Beef, chicken meal, rice flour, maple syrup, rice bran, molasses, beef liver, natural smoke flavor, propylene glycol, salt.

■ **Nutro Chicken and Rice Sticks:** Chicken, chicken meal, rice, maple syrup, natural smoke flavor, propylene glycol, guar gum, salt, garlic powder, potassium sorbate (an artificial preservative).

The maker of tnese two products starts out with good ingredients, so it's unfortunate that they feel it's necessary to add things like propylene glycol, which helps keep the products moist and chewy – do the dogs care? Also, both products lists one natural and one artificial preservative. Too bad they didn't quit while they were ahead.

■ **Ken-L-Ration's Pup-Peroni:** Beef, meat by-products, soy grits, sugar, liver, propylene glycol, natural smoke flavor, garlic powder, caramel color, onion powder. The ingredients here are a step down in quality from those of the Nutro products ("meat by-products" is a step lower on the ladder than chicken meal, and sugar is more refined than molasses) , and they forego using natural preservatives. In our view, two artificial preservatives and at least one artificial color outweighs the benefit of the high beef content.

■ **Purina Beggin' Strips:** Ground wheat, corn gluten meal, wheat flour, ground yellow corn, water, sugar, glycerin, meat, hydrogenated starch hydrolysate, bacon fat preserved with BHA. Beggin' Strips also utilizes three artificial preservatives and four artificial colors.

■ **Ken-L-Ration Snausages:** Soy flour, beef, corn syrup, wheat flour, pregelatinized wheat flour, water sufficient for processing, propylene glycol, cheddar cheese, liver, animal fat. Five different preservatives, four of them artificial, and three artificial colors are utilized to make these treats as attractive as possible – to dog owners!

■ **Ralston-Purina's:** Wheat flour, ground wheat, water, corn gluten meal, beef, sugar, hydrogenated starch hydrolysate, glycerin, dried whey, tricalcium phosphate. Three artificial preservatives and two artificial colors.

■ **Nabisco Inc.'s "Milk Bone Flavor snacks":** If a product as simple as a dog treat has more than 10 ingredients, it probably means its contents aren't much good. After all, these things don't have to sustain a dog for life; they are just a little snack!

But Milk Bone Flavor Snacks contain wheat flour, wheat bran, milled wheat, meat and bone meal, poultry by-product, skim milk, animal fat preserved with BHA, wheat germ, salt, animal liver and glandular meal, vegetable pomace, cheese flavor (containing cereal food fines, dehydrated cheese and soy flour), dried fermented corn extractives (whatever that may be), fish meal, bacon fat, caramel color, brewers dried yeast, malted barley flour, whey, three artificial colors, sodium metabisulfate (a dough conditioner), casein (the principal protein of cow's milk), iron oxide (a coloring agent), and soy lecithin (a natural antioxidant and emollient). This product contains everything we have warned you against.

Considering the toxic burden our dogs must already bear from exposure to a lifetime of vaccinations, insecticides, and de-wormers, it doesn't make any sense to further tax their systems with concentrated doses of additional chemicals, especially artificial preservatives. These are generally used to preserve poor-quality animal fats, which, in turn, are used to attract dogs to products with nutritionally empty fillers. ❖

# 14

# Food Allergies

*While food allergies cannot be cured,
with proper diagnosis and treatment, they can
be managed.*

Food allergies affect 5-10% of dogs, who may develop them after years of eating the same foods. An allergy is a type of immune-system response to a substance the body perceives as "foreign." Because the allergic response builds up over time, a pet may not show symptoms for a long time. When a dog "suddenly" develops a food allergy, he is actually just manifesting symptoms of a condition that has been developing for some time.

Unlike humans, who tend to respond to allergens with sneezing and runny eyes, dogs tend to exhibit skin problems. Commonly skin becomes inflamed and itchy around the feet, face, ears, armpits, and groin. Dogs who rub their faces on the carpet, as well as dogs who have chronic ear infections, may be showing signs of allergy. Some dogs also have gastrointestinal symptoms, such as vomiting and diarrhea.

For example, Chury, a black standard poodle, had always had a delicate digestion. She was choosy about her food, and she occasionally vomited after eating a new brand her owner, Kathy Hayes, would give her. She also suffered from recurrent ear infections. Frustrated, Kathy asked her veterinarian what could be causing Chury's problems. Upon examination, Chury's doctor noticed a thickening of the poodle's ear pinna (outer part). He told Kathy that Chury's troubles might be starting in her food bowl.

However, making a diagnosis that a dog has a food allergy is not a simple matter. Dogs are more commonly allergic to flea bites than to food, and many dogs have seasonal allergies to pollen or to other inhalants. Itchy skin is also a common sign of other conditions such as sarcoptic mange.

# Dietary Changes

Like humans, most dogs who develop allergies are sensitive to a protein in their diet, such as beef, chicken, or dairy products. Because of this, lamb and rice formulas were originally introduced as "hypoallergenic" diets. However, some dogs are allergic to lamb, a reaction veterinarians are seeing more frequently now that lamb-based dog food is widely available. Dogs can also be allergic to proteins in other ingredients, such as corn, soy, or wheat.

Although many pet owners are suspicious of additives like preservatives or coloring, very few dogs are allergic to them. "Allergies to additives are extremely rare," says Dr. Gene Nesbitt, a veterinary dermatologist who is a professor of clinical sciences at Tufts University School of Medicine. "Preservatives are almost never identified as the cause of a food allergy. People think they are, but there's no scientific basis for that belief."

When a food allergy is suspected, some owners are able, like Kathy Hayes, to make a quick fix by switching foods. "I put Chury on a lamb and rice diet," Kathy explains, "and she did much better." However, some dogs are allergic to more than one ingredient in their food. To discover which ingredient is the culprit in a dog's diet, most veterinarians recommend an elimination diet.

The creation of an elimination diet is made individually, based on each dog's food history. Owners must know what sources of protein and carbohydrate their dogs have been exposed to, and they must pick totally new foods to test on their animals. "To really go by the book, home cooking of the elimination diet is the best way to control what a dog is eating," explains Dr. Wendy Brooks, DVM, DABVP, and owner of the Mar Vista Animal Medical Center in West Los Angeles. "But in reality, very few owners want to do that.

"Fortunately, many pet food companies offer diets using unusual protein and carbohydrate sources. There's a fairly new product based on kangaroo meat, as well as diets with venison and rice, fish and potatoes, egg and rice, duck and oat, and more." Your veterinarian may be able to recommend a product for your dog. Some owners, however, opt to cook for their dog during the trial period.

The special diet should be fed for a period up to 10 weeks. Most food-allergic dogs will show improvement by then, although a few breeds, such as Labrador retrievers and cocker spaniels, seem to need longer trials. During that time, only the elimination diet food and water should be consumed—no table scraps, chewies, or biscuits are allowed. Even chewable medications can be a problem. Ask your veterinarian for a capsule or pill form of the dog's drugs.

Most veterinarians like to check on the dog's progress during the elimination diet. If symptoms abate and the dog's condition improves, you can assume that something in your dog's original food caused the condition. However, if you want further proof, you can switch your dog back to his or her original food. Most signs of food allergy will reappear in a week or two.

If the test is successful, many owners simply keep their dogs on the elimination diet they have been using. Some of these specialty diets can be expensive, however, and owners may wish to cautiously introduce different foods to pinpoint the specific ingredient to which their dog is allergic. This is a time-consuming process, as each new food needs to be introduced into the dog's diet over a period of two weeks so that owners may observe any changes in the dog's condition.

Sometimes owners get lucky and find the food quickly. "Chury was allergic to chicken, and every time I served it, she threw it right back up," said Kathy Hayes. Allergies to food coloring or other additives are harder to pinpoint; owners of allergic dogs should probably avoid unnecessary additives altogether.

Others never discover what triggers the allergy but have success nonetheless simply by switching diets. The owners of Annie, a four-year-old Dalmation in Colorado who suffered chronic ear infections, ended all signs of irritation by changing her from a meat protein-based diet to Wysong's Vegan, a vegetarian dry food product.

Sometimes an elimination test is unsuccessful. Owners need to be certain in this case that their dogs have not been eating any other food or substances during the test. (Annie, for a time, skewed the results by eating her housemate's dog food during the night.) At times, veterinarians will ask owners to keep their dogs on a diet for a longer period of time. Further tests may be required, such as a skin biopsy, and a referral to a veterinary dermatologist may also be recommended.

# New Approach: Downsized Proteins

A new trend in the field of canine food allergy focuses on the size of the protein in food—not on the plant or animal source. It may lead veterinarians to diagnose and manage food allergies more quickly and simply. Scientists believe that small proteins are less allergy-provoking than big proteins. "If you chemically cut proteins into smaller molecular chunks, the immune system is less likely to recognize them as foreign substances," explains Steven S. Hannah, Ph.D., a nutrition scientist at Ralston Purina Co. in St. Louis—one of two companies that markets therapeutic canine diets made from small, low-molecular-weight proteins. Purina's CNM-HA Formula uses modified soy protein, while DVM Pharmaceuticals Inc.'s EXclude uses modified protein from casein and liver. Like all therapeutic diets for dogs, both products are available only through veterinarians.

Theoretically, with the "small protein" approach, you don't have to worry about finding novel ingredients. Manufacturers claim that such diets can help veterinarians reliably diagnose food allergies in 4 to 6 weeks. They also claim that you can feed these diets over the long term to manage food allergies—with little or no risk of subsequent allergic reactions.

## Jury Still Out

But before discussing these new therapeutic diets with your veterinarian, remember that many dogs are successfully diagnosed and treated for food allergies using the time-tested elimination-diet technique. Moreover, therapeutic diets don't undergo the rigorous pre-market efficacy testing the U.S. Food and Drug Administration requires of veterinary pharmaceuticals before they are allowed on the market. Caution is also advisable because scientists have only demonstrated the efficacy of low-molecular-weight proteins in the laboratory. Clinical trials in dogs have begun. "There is often a difference between what goes on in a test tube and what goes on in a dog," notes Dr. Lisa Freeman, assistant professor and nutritionist at Tufts University School of Veterinary Medicine.

Your veterinarian will also want to carefully examine the labels of these new diets. He or she will probably pay special attention to the protein content of all the ingredients—not just the major protein source—and check the nutritional adequacy statement. Some therapeutic diets are labeled "intended for intermittent feeding only," meaning they may not be nutritionally adequate for long-term use.

Food allergies can't be cured, but they can be managed successfully by careful feeding. Dogs that are allergic may also develop allergies to their new food, so owners should be prepared for this possibility. In any event, dogs with signs of food allergies should always be evaluated by a veterinarian. ❧

# 15

# Preventing Plump Pooches

*Your "chubster" is beginning to resemble*
*a dirigible, and you're beginning to wonder*
*if he's too fat. Rightly so.*

O besity is the most common nutritional disorder in dogs. By some estimates, at least a quarter of all dogs weigh more than 20 percent over their optimal weight (a common definition of obesity). Although a large proportion of these portly pooches are senior citizens, youngsters are by no means immune to packing on the pounds. Just as in humans, canine obesity contributes to various physical ailments: Obese dogs have a greater incidence of skin disease (dermatosis) than do their svelte counterparts, and have a higher incidence of endocrine disorders (such as diabetes mellitus—a malfunction of the body's glucose-uptake system). And since fat cells need oxygen, too, a fat dog's heart and lungs work harder, exacerbating any existing heart and respiratory conditions. Excess pounds also put extra stress on skeletal joints, aggravating musculoskeletal disease. Furthermore, obese male dogs tend to produce fewer healthy sperm, and pregnant obese dogs have an increased risk of complications during labor (dystocia).

## Recognizing Obesity

Owners often don't notice their pooch's subtle weight gain and don't realize their dog is overweight until a veterinarian, groomer, or trainer points out the extra pounds. Regularly assess your dog's weight to determine whether your pooch needs an adjustment in its feeding and exercise routine. Keeping your dog slim is a lot easier than working to lose weight once the excess pounds have piled up.

You can keep track of your dog's weight by periodically weighing it at a nearby veterinary clinic. You can also assess your animal's body condition with the "rib test." When you stroke your dog's sides, you should be able to easily feel—but not see—the animal's ribs. And when you look at your pooch's silhouette from above, you should be able to see an obvious waistline. If you have difficulty feeling its ribs or seeing its waistline, your dog is overweight. And if you can't feel its ribs at all or see any waistline, your dog is extremely overweight.

# Fatness Factors

Obesity doesn't happen overnight. Typically, a corpulent chow hound has been consuming more calories than it's been expending for months or years. The cause of this imbalanced state of affairs is usually a combination of insufficient energy expenditure—due to lack of physical exercise—and excessive energy consumption—due to eating too much tasty, energy-dense dog food and too many treats.

In addition, a dog's resting metabolic rate (RMR), which determines how many calories the animal expends to maintain normal body functions, may decrease after neutering or spaying. Owners can easily prevent their animal from becoming rotund after spaying or neutering by decreasing its energy consumption and keeping it physically active.

# Slimming Down

If your dog is overweight, your veterinarian can help you determine how many pounds your portly pooch needs to lose. And if the dog shows other signs of illness, the clinician may want to check for a medical disorder—such as hypothyroidism (insufficient thyroid-hormone production)—that could contribute to obesity. You and your veterinarian can work together to develop a weight-loss program that will help your dog gradually shed those extra pounds.

Most successful weight-loss programs employ a three-pronged approach: Decreasing calories; changing the dog's and owner's food-related behavior, and increasing exercise.

■ **Calorie Reduction:** "You definitely need to cut down the number of calories your dog eats, which often means meal feeding as opposed to free-choice feeding," says Dr. Lisa Freeman, assistant pro-fessor and nutritionist at Tufts University School of Veterinary Med-icine. Meal feeding (controlled feeding) is a good idea even if you switch from a regular dog food to a reduced-calorie dog food—be-cause even with a "lite" diet, your dog still runs the risk of con-suming the same (or more) calories by eating larger quantities. You should also be aware that not all low-calorie foods are created equal. Make sure your dog's "low cal" food actually contains fewer calo-ries than the food it had been eating.

■ **Behavior Modification**: We all enjoy praising our dogs, which often includes food treats. But many of our dogs have become con-summate beggars, managing to look ravenous while we prepare and eat our meals. So keeping track of and controlling the amount of calories your dog consumes can be difficult. We recommend you keep begging dogs out of the kitchen during meal preparation and meals. And instead of giving a food treat, give your dog attention and affection.

■ **Increased Exercise**: Regular exercise increases the amount of energy your dog expends. If your pooch is a canine couch potato, start exercising it at a low intensity for short periods of time. Tak-ing it for several short walks each day is a good way to begin. Grad-ually increase the length of your walks and include more intense exercise such as jogging or an energetic game of fetch. If your dog has arthritis or other health problems, talk to your veterinarian about how much exercise is safe for your pet.

If your dog becomes "nudgy" while dieting, try feeding it a low-calorie, high-fiber food. "Some animals may drive their owners less crazy if they are on a high-fiber diet," says Dr. Freeman. You might also try feeding your pooch small amounts of raw carrots; green beans; or unbuttered, air-popped popcorn to satisfy its hunger with-out adding too many calories. And offering more frequent meals (but the same total quantity per day) will help satisfy some dieting pooches. Most of all, when your pooch looks you in the eye with that pitiful gaze, remind yourself that the diet is in your dog's long-term best interest and "stick to your guns."

# Nutrient Deficiencies

Most owners worry more about nutritional deficiency than they do about obesity. But this concern is misplaced since obesity is ex-tremely common, while nutritional deficiencies are extremely rare. "As long as you feed a good-quality commercial diet made by a reputable manufacturer and tested through feeding trials, you are very unlikely to see any deficiencies," says Dr. Freeman. Most commercial foods contain enough vitamins and minerals to meet the needs of the vast majority of dogs. And many manufacturers add extra nutrients to compensate for any possible nutrient loss during storage.

Ironically, owners who are trying to avoid nutritional deficiencies by supplementing with vitamins and minerals may actually cause deficiencies. Too much of one type of vitamin or mineral may interfere with the absorption of another. If your dog or puppy is one of those rare canines with a specific need for an additional nutrient, your veterinarian can advise you on an appropriate supplement.

A dog can also suffer from a nutritional deficiency if its owner feeds it a good-quality commercial food but then adds "people food" such as hamburger. The added topping dilutes and unbalances the nutrients in the commercial diet, which can lead to a nutritional deficiency. Poor-quality commercial food can also cause nutritional deficiency, as can homemade diets. While owners can make their own nutritionally balanced dog food, doing so requires following a carefully formulated scientific recipe that meets a dog's complex nutritional needs. ❧

# 16

# Do Supplements Really Work?

*The jury is still out on whether all dogs need supplements. Be sure your reasons are sound, and buy only the top of the line.*

Diet became hip in the 1990s. People began studying health food and supplements like never before. One nutrient after another was held up as the latest "miracle" herb or vitamin. This one was supposed to give you energy like never before; that one gave you a photographic memory; and then there was the one that practically melted fat off of your bones. Companies sprang up overnight to meet the demand for these "vital" substances.

In almost every case, the initial wave of interest in the products quietly slipped out to sea within a short time. People tried the powders and pills, and, when they failed to effect a dramatic change within a couple or weeks or months, threw away the half-empty bottles.

It was inevitable that a similar movement would come to the canine kingdom. Look in the dog magazines—the ones with ads. You'll see page after page of advertisements for dietary supplements of all kinds. Without fail, all of the ads promise to improve your dog's health. Nine out of ten guarantee to eliminate the single most common complaint of dog owners the world over—itchy, irritated skin. At least half assure the buyer that they will improve the dog's digestion.

Sometimes, the supplements do actually accomplish these things.

When a specific dietary supplement is given to a canine or human who previously lacked the nutrients or chemicals offered by the supplement, or whose body required a higher dose than was previously available, miraculous improvements in health, appearance, and attitude can indeed take place. But most people have no idea whether they are lacking something before they add it to their own or their dog's diet!

# You Need a Reason

There are only two legitimate reasons for supplementing your dog's diet. The **first** and most common need for supplements is to correct a deficiency which has resulted in poor or compromised health, or low vitality or energy.

That said, it should be added that most holistic veterinary nutrition experts agree that many commercially prepared dog foods offer only low-quality sources of nutrients, and that sometimes, the bioavailability of the nutrients is questionable. This alone is enough to make many holistic veterinarians recommend the daily administration of a basic multi-vitamin and mineral supplement to any dog who receives nothing but commercial dog food.

Some holistic veterinarians (and human doctors) believe that much of the world's human food supply is also deficient in vital nutrients, due to intensive modern farming practices. Those people will also recommend the addition of multi-vitamin/mineral combinations to the diet of dogs that are fed an otherwise holistic diet of raw meat and vegetables. The best test of the issue is adding a basic multi vitamin and mineral supplement to your (and your dog's) diet, and taking note of any improvements.

The **second** good reason to add certain supplements to your dog's diet is to strengthen his defenses against an anticipated challenge, such as a stressful long-distance move, competition, lactation, or exposure to infectious disease. For instance, vitamin C is widely recognized for its ability to bolster the immune response, and act as an anti-viral agent.

When a dog with a certain deficiency is given the appropriate nutritional supplement, it can quite literally save his life. The correct supplement can also give a sickly or weak dog increased vigor and a new outlook on life. The difficulty is determining what the dog needs.

No one can make an intelligent decision about what supplement his or her dog needs based on the products' label, advertisements, or web site. If you believe each product's claims, your dog will benefit from each and every supplement on the market. But only a thorough health history intake and examination by a veterinarian, potentially aided by lab tests, can identify nutrient deficiencies. And only the recommendations of an experienced nutrition expert, tailored for your dog, can be considered completely safe and useful.

Obviously, the final decision regarding whether and how you will supplement your dog's diet rests in your hands. Consider the common-sense rules of supplementation below and choose the simplest, good quality supplements you can find

Most important, pay attention to your dog! Note all improvements or declines in his appearance and vitality and adjust your ministrations accordingly.

# Vitamin/Mineral Supplements

Vitamins are complex substances, essential for normal functioning of the body. There are two types: Fat soluble (A, D, E, and K), are stored in fatty tissue and the liver, and water soluble (B and C), which are eliminated daily through the urine. The body can manufacture its own supply of certain vitamins; others need to be supplied by food and other sources. Veterinary nutritionists more or less agree on the amounts of vitamins needed by dogs to stay healthy.

The latter cannot be said for minerals. There is widespread disagreement in the veterinary community regarding what minerals, and in what dosages, are needed for canine health. Scientists only agree that further study is needed, especially regarding dosages for dogs of various breeds and in varying life stages.

Minerals cannot be manufactured by the body. Most people are surprised to learn that mineral deficiencies are more common than vitamin deficiencies. They assist the body in its most critical work, such as energy production, maintenance of electrolytes and fluid balances, and nerve transmission. Trace minerals, including zinc, iron, copper, manganese, cobalt, and iodine, are required by the body only in minute amounts. Here's what we recommend:

■ **Maximum Protection Vitamins & Minerals**: Multi-vitamin and mineral supplementation is generally accepted more readily than supplementation with other nutrients, so it makes sense that there are more brands of multi-vitamin/mineral products on the market than all the other types of supplements put together. Numerous products in this category fit our criteria, but Dr. Goodpet's product stood out from the crowd for a few reasons: First, it comes in a powdered form, enabling you to give your dog an amount tailored to his size; the dosage is one teaspoon per 10 pounds of body weight. The powder also makes it easy to sprinkle on and stir into your dog's food. It includes vitamin C, which is uncommon in the multi-vitamin mixes for dogs. Many veterinarians dispute the idea that dogs need added vitamin C, since their bodies manufacture a certain amount.

Most holistic practitioners, however, acknowledge vitamin C's ability to help the body fight infection and speed healing. Another good thing about Dr. Goodpet's formula is what is *not* in it: preservatives, fillers, anti-caking agents, colors, artificial flavors, or sweeteners.

## Probiotics

*AKA* "friendly bacteria," these substances help the body digest food, and prohibit growth of harmful fungi and microbes in the gut. The most common probiotic supplement is lactobacillus acidophilus, which can actually help the body overcome the yeast and fungal infections that often occur following a treatment of antibiotics.

■ **Canine Digestive Enzymes**: We had a hard time meeting the simplicity requirement on this one. This product is actually a mix of the four major digestive enzymes and lactobacillus. However, we rejected other brands with more expansive "kitchen sink" approaches. PetGuard, for instance, added alfalfa juice powder to their acidophilus product; Pet Authority added yucca, vitamin C, and papaya to theirs. There's no harm in any of those, just complexity.

## Fatty Acids

This term refers collectively to the three substances in fat—linoleic acid, linolenic acid, and arachidonic acid—that contribute the most to the quality of a dog's skin and hair coat. Fatty acids also help prevent cholesterol buildup and heart disease.

■ **Lipiderm**: This is a simple formula, comprised largely of fish oil, and focused on a single purpose. 'Nuf said.

## Digestive Enzymes

An enzyme, in its general definition, is any one of several different proteins that catalyze a biochemical reaction. Each type of enzyme catalyzes only one substance. For instance, protease is an enzyme used by the body to break down protein; amylase works on carbohydrates, lipase on fats, and cellulose on fiber.

These enzymes are present in raw, fresh foods, but are destroyed by the high temperatures needed to manufacture most commercial dog foods. The body produces its own supply of the chemicals, but many nutritionists believe that giving the body additional enzymes (whether in fresh food or in a supplement form) reduces the need for the body to produce the chemicals, lightening the body's workload and speeding the digestive process.

■ **Prozyme**: Sometimes, what you want is what you get. Prozyme contains only the four most important enzymes: lipase, amylase, protease, and cellulose.

# Unique-Source Products

Now we come to a mixed bag of supplements. The products offer vital nutrients, but their makers place more stock in the peculiarity of the nutrient sources than in the nutrients themselves.

■ **Barley Dog** is a good example. The product is not a complete multi-vitamin/mineral supplement; it supplies vitamins A, C, E, B1, B2, and B6, and a few minerals. More significant, say the makers, are the unique qualities of the main ingredient (barley grass), which provide an advantage—a providential synergy—that can't be explained in terms of recommended daily values.

■ **Super Blue Green Algae** (SBGA) takes the cake in the "unique substance" category. We like the product, which is made by Cell Tech, of Klamath Falls, Oregon. SBGA is completely composed of a certain aquatic plant that grows in an Oregon Lake; the algae is collected, freeze dried, and crushed into a fine powder. It contains an array of trace minerals, vitamins B1, B6, B12, C, and D, beta carotene, a number of amino acids, chlorophyll, and nucleic acids, and it's affordable. We've heard great things about the product but dislike that the product is marketed only via independent sales people in-a multi-level marketing system. Critics call the product "glorified pond scum," but to hear it from the converted, SBGA contains almost mystical powers to heal.

# Not Recommended

Some supplements unfortunately fall into our "not recommended" category because of various ingredients we consider artificlal or unnecessary. Some of these include:

■ **Vita-Tabs**: The first ingredient, dextrose, is another word for corn syrup, a sweetener. Considering that the fourth ingredient is molasses, this product is fairly high in sugar, not a supplement that's high on our wish list, but one that certainly contributes to the product's palatability. The need for four different artificial colors in a dog vitamin is a mystery. (Pet Gold Products)

■ **Bene-Pac Pet Gel**: While this product does contain lactobacillus acidophilus and other probiotics, it also contains polysorbate 80, an emulsifier that has been associated with a contaminant that is known to cause cancer in animals; TBHQ, a dangerous antioxidant; and is preserved with ethoxyquin, an antioxidant that has been associated with numerous health problems in dogs. (Pet-Ag, Inc.)

■ **Linatone:** This product has been around a long time, and it has its fans, but we would like to see it eliminate the polysorbate 80, a questionable emulsifier (see Bene-Bac Pet Gel, above). (Lambert Kay)

# Smart Supplementation Tips

■ *If your dog is at the peak of fitness, with a shiny coat and good energy level and no symptoms of ill health— don't change or add anything to his diet! You are already doing a good job!*

■ *Don't give your dog more than the recommended amount of any supplement, especially minerals and fat-soluble vitamins A, D, E, and K. (These nutrients are stored by the body, and can become toxic if used in large doses for a long time.) Accept "radical" or unusual sup-plementation advice only from a veterinarian who has pursued additional training or studies in nutrition.*

■ *Avoid single-nutrient supplementation (adding just calcium, for instance) unless you are working closely with a veterinarian to overcome a demonstrable deficiency. Some nutrients are useful to the body only in proportion to other nutrients, and may actually be harmful if used in a manner that disrupts normal ratios.*

■ *For instance, calcium and phosphorus work favorably for the dog if given in a certain ratio between 1:1 to 1:2. Diet supplementation that alters this ratio can cause the parathyroid glands to try to "fix" the imbalance, by increasing the release of hormones that cause calcium to be drawn from the bones, a phenomenon known as nutri-tional secondary hyperparathyroidism. If your veterinari-an determines your dog needs additional calcium, he will undoubtedly recommend a supplement that offers the nutrient in balance with phosphorus, such as bone meal.*

■ *An exception to the "no single nutrient supplements" rule is water-soluble vitamins such as vitamin C, since the body easily excretes excessive amounts.*

■ *If you want to give your dog more than one type of supplement, you must consult a veterinarian or other professional with experience in nutrition to determine whether the nutrients in the supplements will "overlap," potentially resulting in an overdose of some nutrient or a nutritional imbalance.*

■ *It takes time for nutritional supplements to work. Don't expect to see overwhelming changes within a week or two. But if you can detect no improvement in your dog's appearance, behavior, or vitality within 60 days, the supplement you are feeding is probably unnecessary.*

■ *Abandon any supplementation if your dog's health declines, and consult your veterinarian.*

# You Won't Know Until You Try

Dog owners also get exposed to a number of supplements that contain substances that do not appear on any list of required nutrients. Most are intended as treatments for specific medical disorders. For example, shark cartilage is said (by the makers of a shark cartilage product) to strengthen weak bone and improve joint mobility.

It's easy to dismiss these unusual substances as fads—unless you know a dog that has been helped by one. Who knows? Experimentation with these or other supplements, with the knowledge and support of your holistic veterinarian, just might put a sparkle in your dog's eye and a strut into his step. ♣

# 17

# Canine Diet and Vitamin C

*Nutritionists argue the necessity of*
*adding Vitamin C to*
*the canine diet*

For humans, a source of vitamin C in the diet is literally necessary for survival. Early sailors deprived of fresh foods for extended lengths of time often suffered from "scurvy," a nasty affliction characterized by bleeding gums, loss of teeth, a weakened condition, and sometimes death. It wasn't until the late eighteenth century that Captain James Cook, the first European to visit the Hawaiian Islands, taught the British Admiralty how to prevent scurvy by adding fresh fruit or lime juice to its sailors' daily ration of rum—thus earning them the nickname of "Limeys" that endures to this day.

In the early 1900s, ascorbic acid was isolated and identified as the nutrient that prevented scurvy. Humans, it was discovered, are among the few animals that cannot manufacture vitamin C in their own bodies, and must obtain it from an outside source (fresh fruits, vegetables, or vitamin C pills) on a regular basis in order to avoid illness.

Dogs, however, can produce vitamin C in their bodies, and because of this ability, nutritionists have long considered it unnecessary to add C to a dog's diet. Until recently, few dog food makers added vitamin C to their products—or if they do, it was for the preservative action of the vitamin, rather than its nutritive value.

According to the *Encyclopedia of Nutritional Supplements*, by Michael T. Murray (1996, Prima Publishing), vitamin C improves immune function by enhancing white blood cell function and activity. It also increases the blood levels of interferon (the body's natural antiviral and anticancer compound) and antibodies (proteins that bind to and destroy foreign material such as bacteria, viruses, and toxins).

# Antioxidants and Bioflavonoids

Vitamin C acts in the body as an antioxidant. Oxidation is the chemical reaction of oxygen combining with another substance, and oxidation of food by an animal is a natural process which provides both the heat and the energy needed to keep the body running. Too much or too little oxygen in the system, however, can create toxic by-products called free radicals, which can damage cell structure, impair immunity, and alter DNA codes.

As an antioxidant, vitamin C acts as both an oxygen interceptor (thus protecting the cells from being destroyed or altered by oxidation) and as a scavenger of free radicals. It not only prevents oxidation, but will, for instance, return oxidized vitamin E back to its original state by stealing an oxygen molecule away from the E molecule. Thus vitamin C is a restorative substance that inhibits tissue and collagen degeneration by working in conjunction with the other vitamins and minerals that protect the body and its systems.

As a demonstration of the antioxidant powers of vitamin C, try the following: Dissolve a 1000 milligram tablet of the ascorbic acid form in a large bowl of water. Take some lettuce that has been in the refrigerator a little too long and is getting slightly brown around the edges. Dunk the lettuce in the water for several minutes, then drain it and notice the change. The lettuce should be crisper, fresher and some or all of the brown tinge will be gone. You have just reversed the effects of oxidation! Apple or potato slices can also be dunked in vitamin C solutions to prevent browning. (Anti-browning agents sold for home canning are usually ascorbic acid powder.)

Many types of vitamin C sold also contain bioflavonoids, which are naturally-occurring plant pigments that the body can use to manufacture other nutrients. Beta-carotene, for example, is the bioflavonoid used by the body to manufacture vitamin A. Hesperidin, rutin, acerola, rose hips, citrus bioflavonoids, and bioflavonoid complex are all bioflavonoids commonly used in vitamin C products.

Occasionally supplementing your dog's diet with grated carrots or apples, or offering him any other fresh fruit he finds palatable are great ways to enhance his bioflavonoid intake. Fresh, ripe melons and peaches are two fruits that many dogs enjoy.

# Sickness and Stress

Recent clinical observations indicate that when dogs are sick or stressed, they can rapidly deplete their bodies' output of vitamin C. A 1942 study noted that dogs with skin diseases usually have very low amounts of vitamin C in their blood.

Other researchers have found the blood levels of vitamin C to be low—and even non-existent—in dogs with fevers and dogs who have exercised to their limits (sled dogs after a race, for example, or hunting dogs in the middle of hunting season).

Physical stress comes in many forms: gestation, lactation, growth, hard work (dogs used for herding, hunting, tracking, etc.), vaccinations, injuries, tail-docking or ear cropping, or illness. Emotional stress, whether caused by relocation, weaning, or demanding training, can also deplete this reserve. In fact, researchers can measure the level of stress a dog experiences by measuring the degree of depletion of the vitamin in the dog's blood.

Conversely, many studies have found that dogs (as well as humans) that are supplemented with vitamin C show greater resistance to disease, and a better ability to recover from injuries or illness.

# What C Does for Dogs

Wendell O. Belfield, DVM, is perhaps the world's best-known and most ardent advocate of vitamin C supplementation for dogs. In his book, *How to Have a Healthier Dog*, Belfield describes how he first came to experiment with, and appreciate, the power of vitamin C in his veterinary practice.

Following a particularly heartbreaking episode, where he was unable to save the life of a beloved family dog that had distemper, he began researching viral diseases. In the course of his studies, he came across an article about a doctor who used massive doses of vitamin C to successfully treat viral diseases such as polio and hepatitis in the 1940s. Dr. Belfield began wondering whether C could be used to combat canine viral diseases. One day in 1965, another client came to Belfield's office with a dog that was suffering from distemper. Belfield decided to try an injection of vitamin C on the dog, and it responded dramatically, surviving what he had been taught in veterinary school was a fatal disease for which there is no successful treatments.

Following this success, Belfield began experimenting with vitamin C treatments for all kinds of conditions in dogs. His trials and studies have convinced him of the tremendous power that the vitamin holds for dogs.

# Suggested Uses

Time and further studies are bearing out Belfield's findings. Today, vitamin C is routinely prescribed by holistic veterinarians for a number of illnesses, including cancer, kennel cough and other respiratory infections, abscesses, and other bacterial infections. Due to its important role in maintaining the health of collagen, it appears to be especially helpful for slowing—and some say, reversing—degenerative joint disease, hip dysplasia, and spinal disorders.

The use of vitamin C as a preventative and immune booster are also celebrated. Some veterinarians suggest giving C to dogs before and after vaccination, to dogs that have been exposed to contagious diseases, to pregnant and lactating dogs, and for healthy teeth and gums.

According to Belfield, young dogs and old dogs can benefit the most from routine vitamin C supplements. Due to the extensive stresses faced by puppies and young dogs, such as numerous vaccinations, surgical procedures on dewclaws, tails, and ears, and the demands of rapid growth, he suggests that all young dogs receive C.

As they get old, dogs become less proficient at producing their own supply of vitamin C, and more in need of antioxidants. Administering vitamin C to even very old and feeble dogs, says Belfield, can reinvigorate and strengthen them.Vitamin C is commercially available by itself or combined with other nutrients in a number of forms.

# Dosage

The average dog normally produces about 18 milligrams of vitamin C per pound of body weight per day. Therefore, for a dog that is free of clinically significant symptoms but is experiencing unusual stress, supplementation with about that much C per day appears be a conservative maintenance dosage. (About 500 milligrams for a 28-lb. dog daily.) To increase absorption, veterinarians recommend splitting the total daily dosage into several feedings during the day.

However, many holistic veterinarians routinely suggest maintenance doses that are three to four times that amount., explaining that modern, domestic dogs need more vitamin C than the theoretical "natural" dog, since their bodies must deal with so many challenges, including: stress, pollution, chemicals and pesticides, and poor diets.

CANINE DIET AND VITAMIN C ■ 121

Too much vitamin C, especially if given in one dose, will cause diarrhea in dogs. What amount is too much varies from dog to dog, so, when administering the maximum amount of C for a therapeutic (not just maintenance) dose, many veterinarians will suggest that you increase the dose in 100-500 milligram-per-day increments until the dog develops diarrhea, then reduce his daily dose to the previous day's dose—often referred to as dosing to "bowel tolerance."

A HEALTHY, HAPPY DOG WITH A QUALITY DIET AND LITTLE STRESS PROBABLY HAS NO NEED OF SUPPLEMENTATION WITH VITAMIN C.

Individuals dogs may be more or less tolerant of vitamin C supplements, and their tolerance may change with environmental conditions. For instance, a dog that is experiencing great stress may tolerate 4,000 milligrams without diarrhea, but develop the condition as the stress is removed. The owner's awareness of the quality of the dog's stool is critical to appropriate dosing.

The type of illness being treated should also be considered when determining the dose. Some guidelines published by holistic veterinarians include: Richard Pitcairn, DVM, *Dr. Pitcairn's Complete Guide to Natural Health for Dogs and Cats*. Pitcairn suggests giving 100-500 milligrams, based on the dog's size, of vitamin C daily to dogs that are exposed to unusually high amounts of pollutants.

Cheryl Schwartz, DVM, *Four Paws, Five Directions: A Guide to Chinese Medicine for Cats and Dogs*. Schwartz suggests giving vitamin C to dogs with a variety of illnesses, including upper respiratory conditions (small dogs, 125 to 500 mg. twice daily; medium dogs, 250-1,500 mg. twice daily; large dogs, 500-1,500 mg. twice daily), arthritis (to bowel tolerance), infected ears (small dogs, 250-500 mg. twice daily; large dogs, 500-1,000 mg. twice daily), and skin allergies (small dogs, 125 mg. twice daily; medium and large dogs, up to 750 mg. twice daily).

It's important to remember that a healthy, happy dog with a quality diet and little stress probably has no need of supplementation with vitamin C. However, if stress, illness, or age causes a dog's need for vitamin C to outstrip his ability to produce it, supplementing him with C is a sensible choice.

# What Form of Vitamin C Is Best?

Assuming you have a dog that would benefit from vitamin C supplementation, what options are there? Many vitamin C supplements labeled and sold specifically for dogs use ascorbic acid, the only naturally occurring form of vitamin C.

Unfortunately, among all the vitamin C supplements on the market, ascorbic acid has the poorest absorption rate by the body. However, the salt forms of vitamin C, known as ascorbates, are easily absorbed in the intestinal tract of humans, dogs, and other mammals.

For dogs, the sodium ascorbate form of vitamin C appears to be the best choices in terms of cost, bioavailability, and effectiveness. However, be aware of the differences between the various forms.

■ **Ascorbic Acid**: This is the naturally occurring form of vitamin C. A tart-tasting organic acid (pH 2.5-3.0) in crystalline form, this is the form of vitamin C most frequently used in vitamin C pills for humans. When given in high concentrations or in single large doses, however, ascorbic acid is not efficiently absorbed by dogs or humans and can cause diarrhea. Using smaller doses several times a day can alleviate this symptom. Most dogs find powdered forms of ascorbic acid to be unpalatable due to its tartness.

■ **Ascorbyl Palmitate**: Although vitamin C is considered a water-soluble vitamin, an oil-soluble form called ascorbyl palmitate is also available, and is thought to act synergistically with other antioxidants. Although oral administration of this form is three times more efficient than the ascorbic acid form, ascorbyl palmitate costs about six times as much as ascorbic acid.

■ **Calcium Ascorbate**: Vitamin C can also come in the form of salts called mineral ascorbates (compounds formed by replacing all or part of the hydrogen ions of an acid with one or more metallic ions). These forms of vitamin C—known as calcium ascorbate and sodium ascorbate—are easily absorbed anywhere in the human intestinal tract and in that of most mammals. These are thought to be the most gentle (buffered) forms of vitamin C and cause the fewest side effects such as diarrhea or heartburn.

Calcium ascorbate, a pH-neutral, slightly bitter powder, is one commercially available mineral ascorbate. Many health practitioners are of the opinion that calcium ascorbate gives the best results in the relief of arthritic symptoms. It is also considered by holistic veterinarians to be the most beneficial form of vitamin C for use in horses.

■ **Ester C Calcium Ascorbate:** Most of the results which have been published regarding the use of vitamin C in horses and dogs have been in trials using a patented form of C known as Ester C calcium ascorbate. Like the pure forms of calcium and sodium ascorbate, Ester-C is non-acidic with a neutral pH and does not cause gastrointestinal upset. This product is the result of a unique method of manufacturing mineral ascorbates, which yields what are called metabolites as well as the minerals and the ascorbates. Thus, Ester C calcium ascorbate is a combination of calcium, ascorbate, and metabolites (including a substance known as threonate).

Pure calcium ascorbate is simply calcium and ascorbate. Pure sodium ascorbate is sodium and ascorbate. When these and all other forms of vitamin C are processed in the body, metabolites (including threonate) are naturally occurring products. The patent holder of the Ester C brand, Intercal Corporation, claims the presence of metabolites, especially threonate, in their product before intake into the body increases cellular absorption and longevity of vitamin C in the bloodstream.

*It's easy to get confused when contemplating the many vitamin C products available. For best results, easiest administration and palatability, we suggest using a powdered form of pure sodium ascorbate.*

However, these observations were made when the product was compared to ascorbic acid. The company has not released results of studies (if there are any) comparing Ester C directly to the pure forms of calcium and sodium ascorbate.

■ **Sodium Ascorbate**: Readily available and easily absorbed, sodium ascorbate is a pH-neutral granular powder with a slightly saline taste. Sodium ascorbate is easily absorbed by the body, and studies have also shown that it stays in the system twice as long as the acid form. It is the only form of vitamin C approved by the FDA for intravenous injection in humans. It is also the preferred form for oral megadoses in humans because it does not irritate the intestinal tract and the excess is easily eliminated without harm to the kidneys

# Purest Product/Best Price

Once you decide on which form of vitamin C you want, the least expensive sources are usually mail-order distributors that sell vitamins for human consumption. Here are some tips.

1) For the best price on the active ingredient, purchase "pure" vitamin C products. Skip products with added ingredients such as bioflavonoids and vegetable fillers. Bioflavonoids may be listed as bioflavonoid complex, rutin, hesperidin, rose hips, and acerola.

2) Look for product listed as USP pure. USP stands for United States Pharmacopoeia and refers to a list of standards established by the FDA governing methods of manufacture and degree of purity for products designated pharmaceutical grade.

3) For ease in feeding, use a powder or crystal form. On average, one teaspoon of pure powder or crystals contains five grams (5,000 milligrams) of vitamin C, so an average maintenance dose for a healthy dog will be 1/8 - 1/4 of a teaspoon. Tablets are sometimes less expensive, but you will have to grind them up or find a way to get your dog to swallow them.

4) To compare prices you need a standard unit to compare. Manufacturers sometimes use different units of measure, but grams are the most common. You'll have to do some converting to be able to compare prices, and obviously, this will only be applicable to pure forms of the vitamin, not mixed with any other nutrients or fillers.

At one source, we were quoted $26 for 21.34 ounces of pure calcium ascorbate. There are 28.35 grams in one ounce. Multiply 21.34 ounces by 28.35 grams per ounce; this bottle contains 605 grams. Divide $26 for the bottle by 605 grams of calcium ascorbate; the product costs 4.3 cents per gram. ❧

# Section II

---

# Care

# 18

# What We Do for Our Dogs!

*Whatever you do to keep your "best friend" comfy—*
*special treats or his favorite radio station—*
*you're not alone.*

Considering that our dogs freely give us unconditional loyalty, protection, entertainment, and much-needed diversion from life's stresses, it's no wonder owners go to great lengths to make life healthy and happy for their dogs. Let's look at some of the "above and beyond" steps people take to promote the well-being of their canine companions.

## ■ Enriched environments:

Many owners provide creative forms of stimulation for dogs they must leave "home alone" from time to time. Such environmental enrichment often takes the form of leaving televisions and radios on. Tufts University School of Veterinary Medicine took an informal poll and found that classical music and talk shows are the most popular listening choices. (But keep the volume down because dogs have much more acute hearing than we do.)

To provide even more realistic "company," you could play a continuous-loop audiotape of household voices and noises for your dog when it's alone, suggests Dr. Nicholas Dodman, director of the Behavior Clinic at Tufts University School of Veterinary Medicine.

Dogs are ever interested in what's going on around them. If your dog is not excessively protective or predatory, give your home-alone pooch opportunities to look outside. To facilitate this, move a step stool or piece of furniture (one that can withstand some wear, tear, and hair!) close to a window. Some owners have been known to

build in dog-friendly windows. Phyllis and Leo Mikolaiczik of St. Helen, Michigan, report that they had already started construction on their new home when they rescued their cairn terrier Toto. "We changed the design scheme so the windows would be installed 12 inches from the floor, allowing Toto to look out," recalls Phyllis.

Leash walking is ordinarily one of the best ways to exercise and stimulate your dog, but sometimes this commonplace activity is a bit more complicated than one would expect. Dr. Linda Ross, hospital director at Tufts University School of Veterinary Medicine, tells of one owner who adopted a dog with a congenital heart defect, which made even mild exercise risky. "When this woman walks her group of dogs, she puts the one with the heart condition in a baby stroller," says Dr. Ross.

## ■ Behavioral bonuses:

Some owners who have dogs with behavioral problems go to great (and innovative) lengths to help their pets. In the title chapter of *The Dog Who Loved Too Much*, Dr. Dodman recounts the story of Elsa, a Labrador retriever with separation anxiety. To help Elsa handle solitude more calmly, her resourceful owner made a continuous-loop audiotape of himself issuing obedience commands and enthusiastic praise. He then added a voice-activated circuit so the tape ran only when Elsa began whimpering with anxiety. When Elsa heard her owner's voice, she calmed down.

## ■ Medical management:

Many owners go the extra mile, emotionally and financially to help dogs manage chronic, incurable canine conditions like epilepsy and diabetes. Even less-serious chronic conditions, such as allergies, move some owners to take extraordinary measures like removing carpet to cut down on dust mites.

## ■ Special menus:

Owners also often make culinary accommodations for their dogs. Every day, Dr. Bruce Fogle, a London-based veterinarian, prepares rotisserie chicken and fettucine with olive oil for his 14-year-old golden retriever Liberty, whose heart condition has led to appetite loss and cardiac cachexia—severe muscle wasting. While he does his best to balance the nutrients in this homemade diet, Dr. Fogle is more concerned that Libby eats than he is with concocting a completely balanced diet—a greater concern if Libby were a younger dog with a longer life expectancy. The biggest problem: friends sometimes find the dog's food in the fridge and unwittingly eat it.

## ■ Creature comforts:

Sometimes, we take special measures just to make canine life more pleasurable. When selecting cars, dog people often place greater stock in easy canine access and their dog's interior-space requirements than they do in power and styling. (Some owners even bring their dogs along for test drives.)

Greta, one of our loyal dog consultants, is blessed with owners who put her comfort first. The 8-year-old Saint Bernard with chronic arthritis has four beds, each strategically placed in one of her favorite lying-down places. Greta's owners know a Saint can drain a standard-sized water bowl in two slurps, so Greta has two large buckets of fresh water in the kitchen, one in the bathroom, and one in the garage—her favorite hangout in hot weather. And when Greta's "dad" was assembling a workbench in the garage, he purposely left off the lower shelf to avoid interfering with the big dog's favorite snoozing spot.

Finally, we heard about an owner who paid her housecleaner extra to perform a slightly unusual task—vacuuming the dog, who relished that kind of grooming.

# The Results Are In

*According to a recent survey conducted by the American Animal Hospital Association, owners of home-alone pets go to great lengths to assure their animals' comfort and safety. Specifically:*

*60% of pet owners leave the air conditioner or fan on.*
*50% leave toys out for their pets.*
*41% leave lights on.*
*32% turn on the TV or radio.*
*30% open windows or blinds.* ❣

# 19

# How Safe is Your Home?

*We suggest 10 ways to reduce toxins
in and around your house.
It's a start!*

Admit it: If you thought that conditions in your house were dangerous to your health, you would change them or move. The same holds true for your canine pals. And yet many of us expose our beloved friends to life-threatening toxins and life-shortening conditions.

Many of the dangers lurk in products we use casually, without knowledge of their effects on our dogs. Ironically, while some of these conditions are potential threats to our own health, we often fail to consider them until they wreak havoc with the vitality of one of our animals.

Many of these hazards are chemical in nature. Exposed on a daily basis, our pets bear ever-increasing loads of toxins, from the lawns and yards they romp in which are often treated with pesticides and fertilizers, to the sidewalks and streets where we walk them and, too often, even the rugs and floors they lie in our own homes. Holistic veterinarians theorize that this constant bombardment of toxins, paired with unhealthy diets and over-zealous vaccination schedules, results in the rampant allergies and autoimmune dysfunctions so commonly seen in today's dogs.

Fortunately, we can easily improve the health conditions in our homes. What follows is a list of 10 commonly found household health hazards. Reducing your dog's, and your own, exposure to as many of them as possible can improve your health, and maybe even extend your lives together.

# ■ Toxic cleaners

If used in total accordance with the cautions on their labels, few household cleaners are dangerous to your dog. The problem is, many people never read or ignore the labels. Never mind that this is a violation of federal law—what you don't know can hurt your dog. Our first recommendation: **Read the label.**

A note about hazard warnings: If the hazard begins, "Caution," or "Warning," it signals that the product is not likely to produce permanent damage as a result of exposure, if appropriate first aid is given. If the hazard begins, "Danger," it indicates that even greater precautions should be taken, since accidental exposure or ingestion could cause tissue damage. Examine the labels of all your household products to determine the level of caution you should employ when using the product—or whether to use it at all.

To avoid accidentally poisoning your dog, never leave a bucket or bowl containing any cleaning solution unattended. If you mix cleaners into any container that resembles one your dog has drunk from, make sure you empty and rinse it well before you walk from its view. If you pour bleach or other cleaners into your toilet bowl, make sure you close the lid.

Never mix cleaning products. Products that are safe when used alone can sometimes become dangerous when mixed with other products. A common mishap occurs when people unwittingly mix products containing bleach (sodium hypochlorite) with products containing ammonia or acids. Such mixtures will release highly dangerous gases.

The safest approach to housecleaning? Look for products that carry the "Green Seal of Approval." To earn a Green Seal, a product must pass rigorous tests and meet the most stringent environmental standards. Green Seal products must demonstrably reduce air and water pollution, cut the waste of energy and natural resources, slow ozone depletion and the risk of global warming, prevent toxic contamination, and protect fish and wildlife and their habitats. See Appendix.

# ■ Poisonous plants

Many common house and garden plants are highly poisonous if consumed. Few dogs eat plants, but you never know! Bored or agitated canines have done strange things. The following plants are dangerous to dogs: All plant parts **Azaleas, buttercup, calla lily, laurels, rhododendron, tiger lily, philodendrons, poinsettia, mistletoe. Bulbs: crocus, daffodil, tulip.** Berries: Christmas berry, jasmine, red sage.

The best course is to eliminate poisonous plants from your home decorating and landscaping plans.

*Read the labels of all your household products to determine the level of caution you should employ when using the product—or whether you should use it at all.*

## ■ Cigarette smoke

Everyone knows about the dangers of secondhand smoke for humans. Not everyone has thought about it enough to realize that cigarette smoke is just as dangerous to dogs as it is to humans. If you don't want to shorten your dog's life, consider quitting or smoking outdoors only. Ask guests to smoke outside, too.

## ■ Hazardous chewable items

If you have a teething puppy or a dog that has gotten into the habit of chewing odd items, you should dog-proof his environment as stringently as you would for a baby. While it is impossible to eliminate every single item that might be dangerous if chewed, remove all the likely suspects from his reach: electric cords, medicines, cleaners, and chemical containers. If the dog cannot be kept under observation, he should be contained in a puppy pen or crate with a few appropriate chew toys.

## ■ Chemical flea controls

Fleas are annoying. They can make you and your dog near-crazy with itching, transmit larvae for tapeworms, and aggravate allergies. But when we're locked in a battle for control over a rampant flea population, we tend to go overboard, enlisting the aid of any and every chemical known to science—pet sprays, collars, shampoos, powders, dips, and tablets, as well as chemical sprays applied to our rugs, floors, and even yards.

Unfortunately, many of the products on the market are quite toxic to the pets they are trying to protect. Organochlorines, found in some flea dips and shampoos, can cause exaggerated responses to touch, light and sound, spasms and muscle tremors, and seizures. Carbamates, found in dips, collars, powders, and sprays, can cause profuse salivation, muscular twitching, slowed pulse, labored breathing, vomiting, watery eyes, and paralysis, to name but a few symptoms. Pyrethrins, derived from chrysanthemums and thus often considered "natural," are the least toxic chemicals commonly used in flea shampoos and sprays, but to be effective, they require far more frequent applications.

Read the labels carefully. When a label tells you to avoid getting the product on your own skin, to wash it off quickly and thoroughly, to avoid breathing the fumes, and to dispose of the empty container in a certain manner, it's telling you that the product is really not that "safe." Can it really be "harmless" for your dog?

## ■ Dirty water

Plenty of fresh, clean, cool drinking water must always be available to your dog. Dehydration can cause and worsen many other health conditions. An ample supply of good water, on the other hand, can help the dog's body shed environmental toxins.

To ensure your dog wants to drink water, put the bowl in a cool, protected place where dust and debris won't fall in it, keep the bowl clean, and keep the water fresh and cool. If your tap water smells bad or contains any substances that have moved you to buying pure drinking water for your family, provide the good drinking water for your dog, too.

## ■ Garden chemicals

Dogs absorb insecticides, herbicides, and fungicides from the soil by walking, lying, and rolling on it. They are also exposed to many potent insecticides in the home, like ant, roach, or fly sprays. Long-term exposure to these chemicals decreases the vitality of the animal by taxing the organ and glandular function, and increases the animal's chances of suffering from cancer, allergies, and kidney and liver problems. Signs that an animal's body is working overtime to rid itself of toxins include oily, smelly secretions on the skin and in the ears, and excessive eye "goop."

Outside, use native species of plants in your garden; they will naturally resist many local pests. Alternatively, plant disease-resistant strains of plants, flowers, trees, and vegetables, available at most nurseries. The health of these strains is less-dependent on the use of chemicals. Use "friendly" enemies of pests, like ladybugs, which hungrily consume the aphids that plague roses and other plants. Ask your neighbors about their pesticide use, and let them know about your most successful organic gardening techniques.

Also, if you have to use solvent, paints, or harsh cleaners in your home or garage, dispose of the waste by soaking it up with rags, sand, or cat litter, and disposing in a garbage can. Don't just sweep or hose the chemicals into the soil or onto the lawn. Contrary to appearances, the chemical don't just disappear.

Indoors, use good housekeeping practices to control pests. Keep floors and counters wiped clean and empty your kitchen garbage can frequently.

REDUCING YOUR DOG'S, AND YOUR OWN, EXPOSURE TO AS MANY (TOXINS) AS POSSIBLE CAN IMPROVE YOUR HEALTH, AND MAYBE EVEN EXTEND YOUR LIVES TOGETHER.

## ■ Air "fresheners"

Contrary to popular belief, commercial air and carpet deodorizers don't work by somehow making the air and the carpet smell better. Rather, they work by making you smell worse—by (temporarily) deadening the nerves associated with your sense of smell. They also use strongly perfumes to overwhelm other odors that may be present. This must be difficult for our dogs to cope with, considering their sense of smell is about 40 times more powerful than our own.

To genuinely freshen a room's odor, sprinkle baking soda liberally on carpets. Vacuum it up after 30 minutes or so. Vanilla extract, poured into a shallow dish on a high shelf where Fido can't reach it, can make a room smell good.

# ■ Carpet shampoo

Most formulas of carpet cleaning liquids contain either per-chlorethylene, a known carcinogen that damages the nervous system and liver and kidney tissues, or ammonium hydroxide, a corrosive agent that is extremely irritating to eyes, skin, and respiratory passages.

If you rent a carpet cleaner, try using plain hot water, which works very well all by itself to remove dirt and odors from rugs. You'll probably be amazed at the amount of soap suds in the dirty water you empty from the cleaning tank when you're done. These residues are evidence of the chemicals that have lurked in the carpet since the last time it was cleaned.

# ■ No emergency plan?

Natural disasters can and do strike anywhere, anytime. In the mass confusion following a fire, earthquake, flood, mudslide, snowstorm, or hurricane, our animal friends can easily get lost or separated. Another disaster can happen if any of the above calamities cuts off your food and water supply.

Store provisions for your pets along with your family's emergency supplies. Disaster preparedness experts recommend keeping at least a two-week supply of food and water for both the humans and animals in the house. Canned and dry foods should be stored (along with a can opener!) in a cool, dry place. Be sure to check the dated shelf life, occasionally buying new stocks and using the stored goods. Keep at least 10 gallons of water on hand, rotating and using the bottles so that none are stored for more than a couple of months.

Having identification on your animal friend may be his only chance to be returned to you if he gets lost in a disaster. Even if the phone (or even the house at the address!) listed on your dog's ID tags is missing after a disaster, the information can be used by rescuers to reunite you with your beloved friend. It can also be a good idea to keep a good photo of your dog with your most important papers, the kind of papers you'd grab first if you had to run out of your house in an emergency. The photo should clearly show the dog's size and markings. ❖

# 20

# Five Steps to Fitness

*Continuing attention to these simple steps
will promote lifelong wellness
for your dog.*

Everyone knows there are many different ways we can become healthier. We can change our diets, systems of medicine, exercise plans, and environment in order to improve our physical, mental, emotional, and spiritual well-being. We're aware that what works for our sister or co-worker may not work for us. At times, we may have to work a little hard in order to find our own solutions to health problems.

So why do we so often place the health and well-being of our canine friends solely into the hands of our veterinarians, blindly following their prescriptions for diet, exercise, vaccinations, and medication? We've all met people who do not vaccinate their children at all, but vaccinate their animals for eight diseases annually. Or people who won't eat anything but the freshest, most organic food they can afford, but feed canned or dry food to their dogs. Many, even alternative health care practitioners, take their animals to a good veterinarian and follow their directions implicitly, even if they contradict our personal philosophies. We treat whatever symptoms the animal exhibits with whatever the veterinarian recommends—something we wouldn't dream of doing for our own medical conditions.

It's time to realize there are just as many options for improving our dog's health as there are for our own. It's not difficult. If you look at the big picture—the holistic approach—and make small but significant changes in a number of aspects of how you care for your dog, he will live a longer, more vibrant life.

# Five Basic Areas

By looking in five basic areas, you can discover what your dog needs to be glowingly healthy, keeping in mind,that each dog in your household may need a different approach.

- Diet
- Vaccination
- Environment
- Best treatment modality
- Most effective practitioner

Any time you take a new approach, start by evaluating your dog's health, past and current. You may want to start a journal that describes his current health condition, so you can re-evaluate readily in the future.

## ■ Diet

Some veterinarians and holistic practitioners believe the best diet for dogs is raw meat, including raw bones, grated raw and cooked vegetables, and maybe some grains, seeds, nuts, and supplements. We all know that it's best to use fresh, organic vegetables and meat from free-ranging holistically treated animals. Get the best that you can afford. Ask for scraps, meat just at its expiration date, and left-overs from meals out (a real doggy bag).

There are a number of approaches and differences of opinion regarding animal nutrition. Choose an approach based on what makes the most sense to you, and give it a try. One caution: Do not stray too far from the basic guidelines. There are some healthy dogs that are fed an exclusively vegetarian diet, but most of the healthy ones self-selected the diet rather that having their owners impose one. Most dogs need at least 25 percent meat; some need up to 60 percent or even more.

Wait, you say, what about canned or dry animal foods? I think most people would agree that they couldn't possibly feel their best if they ate only instant breakfasts and military K rations. But why not, since those foods meet the Minimum Daily Requirements?

Because all animals do better if fed a variety of fresh foods, in our opinion, even if it is less convenient to buy raw meat than to bring home 50-lb. sacks of dried food. If you are truly interested in bringing your dog to optimum health, you'll make the switch. It's not the easiest task, but countless dogs have health and behavior problems that appear to be linked to poor diet. It's worth doing.

## Chambreau's Quality Diet Scale

**90** ......*Raising your own produce and meat*

**80** ........*Fresh from organic sources*

**40** ........*Fresh from the grocery store*

**5** ..........*Processed canned or dry foods with very good ingredients (the problem is that the meat here is cooked and not in big chunks to exercise the jaw and teeth ligaments)*

**-50** ......*Processed canned or dry foods with artificial preservatives, colors, flavors, and poor quality ingredients*

## ■ Vaccinations

Apply the same thinking you have about vaccinations for people to your animal friends. How many of you receive a polio, diphtheria, measles, mumps, and hepatitis vaccination every year of your life till you die? Your dog is probably getting vaccinated for Distemper, Hepatitis, Leptospirosis, Parainfluenza, and Parvo virus all in the one "annual booster", and may also be getting Bordetella (kennel cough), Coronavirus, and Lyme vaccines yearly, as well as the legally required Rabies vaccine every one to three years.

Researchers in conventional veterinary medicine agree that we vaccinate too often, in too many combinations, and that this level of vaccination, while often preventing epidemics, is harmful to the health of susceptible animals. Holistically, we find vaccinations one of the most harmful things for our animals. Many strong, healthy animals, of course, are not bothered by poor nutrition or vaccination. Unfortunately, there is ample evidence that these animals are the exception, not the rule, in the domestic dog population today.

Dr. Jean Dodds, famed for her work in autoimmune problems of specific breeds, asserts that hypothyroidism, bleeding disorders, multiple autoimmune problems (including allergies), some cancers, and many other problems are due to over-vaccination in susceptible breeds. Drs. Macy, Schultz, Carmichael, Tizzard, Frick and others have stated that we do not know how frequently to vaccinate and that many animals seem adversely affected by vaccines. Many of these veterinarians vaccinate their own dogs for Distemper and Parvo only, and then only as pups.

Holistic veterinarians are finding that vaccines are causing great harm to our animals. To cure an animal we must use homeopathic remedies known to reverse vaccine-related problems that include chronically draining eyes, anal gland difficulties, dull hair coat, chronic otitis, diabetes, and more. These conditions are often arrested following use of appropriate homeopathic remedies, but equally often recur if more vaccinations are given during treatment.

The inserts that come with all vaccines say to use them only on healthy animals. So, once an animal has glowing health, why vaccinate?

Healthy animals have broad, non-specific immunity that will allow them to respond appropriately to most infections. If they do get an infectious disease, your holistic practitioner may have more success treating the acute problem than the chronic sequellae to vaccines. Read all you can on this topic and make your own decision rather than letting your veterinarian, holistic or conventional, decide for you.

# ■ Environment

What is the best environment for your dog? Again, each animal is different, just like each child is different. Some children can go to any school and do well, while others must try out several schools before finding the learning situation that is best for them. There is no single correct answer.

Some dogs, even when very healthy, are basically couch potatoes, enjoying only moderate walks or short spells of ball chasing. Asking these dogs to go on 10-mile hikes every weekend may cause physical problems, even if they acquiesce in order to please you. Active, athletic dogs will suffer if they are forced to live in an environment that permits them little exercise, or with a person who restricts their exercise. Sen-

sitive dogs with autoimmune disorders or chemical sensitivities may not be able to thrive in a polluted urban environment. High-strung dogs may not be cut out for life in a home filled with rambunctious young children, or, conversely, an outgoing dog who desires stimulation and contact with people may wilt and decline if left home alone for long periods of time.

Even when we do not have the perfect environment for our animals, we can try to do our best by them by stopping and thinking about what is needed.

If you are unable to provide the best environment, do not fret. Your dog will thrive on your love and knowing that you are trying your best.

# Indications of Poor Health (Often Mistaken as "Normal")

■ *Skin: Doggy smell (dogs should not need a bath to smell nice, unless they roll in something or get muddy), attracts fleas a lot, dry coat, oily coat, lackluster coat, excessive shedding, chronic ear problems (excessive ear wax), eye discharge, tearing, or matter in corner of eyes.*

■ *Behavior: Fear of loud noises, thunder, wind; barking too much and too long, suspicious nature, timidity; excessively licking things or people, irritability, indolence, eating dog stool (especially cat stool; it seems to be normal for dogs to eat horse, cow, and rabbit manure), feet sensitive to handling, aggressiveness at play, destructiveness, slow to learn, lack of playfulness and alertness.*

■ *Digestive: Mucous on stools, even occasionally, tendency to diarrhea with least change of diet, constipation, obesity, bad breath, poor appetite, craving weird things, especially non-food items like plastic or paper, teeth and gum problems.*

■ *Stiffness: when getting up, early hip dysplasia.*

■ *Temperature: Sensitive to heat or cold. Low grade fevers (normal temperature for dogs is 100-101.5).*

# ■ Supporting health

Your dog is capable, to a certain extent, of healing himself, just as you are capable of assisting in your own healing process. To develop and take advantage of this natural phenomenon, simply seek out ways that you can improve his health, rather than merely treating each disorder or symptom of ill health. Again, there is no one right method of treatment. Some (although very few) animals simply do not enjoy acupuncture, some animals do not exhibit the characteristic idiosyncrasies we need to prescribe homeopathic remedies, and some thrive when they receive the energy support of Reike or therapeutic touch. Most will improve with any proficient treatment.

THERE ARE JUST AS MANY OPTIONS FOR

IMPROVING OUR DOG'S HEALTH AS THERE

ARE FOR OUR OWN.

Many people consider their animals to be "healthy" as long as they aren't sick. To me, a healthy dog is one that is positively glowing and vibrant. He appears to be happy and expressive, and exudes resilience.

On the other hand, there are many things that our dogs do that we consider normal but that are actually early warning signs of unhealth (see chart, above). These and other symptoms are clues as to the level of your dog's health and indications of the success of whatever treatment you choose.

Healthy animals can, and do, get "sick" occasionally, with acute symptoms that resolve quickly with minimal treatments. Finding the combination of treatments that will support a person or animal to heal itself can be challenging. Today's culture is full of recommendations that undermine our best efforts to truly heal—"Get rid of your cough quickly and get back to work." "Take these pain pills and you can work all day." "Give your dog these steroids and he will stop scratching today."

Finally, consider the fact that sometimes, doing less is more. Not every abnormal symptom needs to be gotten rid of as if it were the sole reason for your dog's ill health. When your dog has diarrhea, for instance, traditional veterinarians and holistic veterinarians alike could give your dog something to stop the diarrhea. Alternatively, you could wait a few days, observe the diarrhea, rest the dog, give him a very mild, soothing intestinal treatment like aloe vera or slippery elm, and fast your dog. Even holistically, we often jump too fast to treat problems. "Tincture of time" is often the best remedy.

Make a plan for your healthy dog. Attend courses. Choose holistic animal practitioners to work with. Visit them or speak with them to learn how to keep your dog healthy. If your dog does get sick, ask yourself whether a little TLC, fasting, or diet change would help.

You have a choice for your dog and yourself. One is to quickly get rid of symptoms, even at the cost to his overall health. The other is to begin the journey to health and explore the different options, tolerating symptoms while slowly building up your dog's overall health. If one treatment doesn't help, move on to the next—or onto another practitioner.

## ■ Use the most effective practitioners

You, not your veterinarian, are responsible for your animal's health.

It may be attractive to simply turn over all your decisions to someone else, but it is not best for your dog. Pay attention to what works for your dog and what does not work. You may have a wonderful veterinary acupuncturist who thinks you should feed canned food. You certainly can use her for acupuncture, but follow your heart and feed raw meat! Observe your dog closely, and stand firm with the regimen that you can see working for him. If something is not working, even if it is a treatment you have a lot of faith in, you have to stay open to the possibility that it isn't right for that individual animal at that specific time. Be flexible enough to admit it when you (or your practitioner) makes a mistake, and keep trying to find something that does work!

If it seems to you that a practitioner's approach to your dog's health problem is palliating (symptoms keep coming back and your dog is no healthier overall) or being suppressed (symptoms do not come back, but the dog is sicker than before in other ways), rather than curing the underlying cause, talk to him or her about your concerns. He may want to work with you to develop another approach to the problem, refer you to another professional, or you may decide to choose your next option. Read, talk to other people, and discuss your issues with your animal health care providers. Be nice to them and they will be nice to you.

The path to health for your animals can be fun and challenging. Your dog will love your experimentation with all the different forms of healing.

# Western vs Holistic Approaches

Holistic modalities are those that treat the entire animal (or person) rather than just trying to get rid of one symptom at the cost of weakening the overall life force. (Caution: not every practitioner who calls himself "holistic" actually practices that way.)

Every individual is born with a unique energy field that has weak areas and/or susceptibilities to diseases. When animals get sick we try to help them by addressing the symptoms. We may use anti-inflammatories and antibiotics, or acupuncture points, herbs, or homeopathic remedies, but in each case, we often choose the remedy for the symptoms rather than the individual. While any of these treatment modalities (or any others) can eliminate the symptoms, usually the animal is not healthier overall. They are simply not exhibiting the specific symptom we treated (and which will probably recur). We now know it is possible to treat people and animals so that they become healthier on many levels and stay that way.

Traditional Western medicine tends to view individuals as healthy unless they have symptoms; if they do, then practitioners are quickly called on to eliminate the "sick" symptom. On the other hand, it's a basic tenet of holistic medicine that the bodies of living organisms are always striving to be healthy, and that "sick" symptoms are the body's best attempt to heal an underlying imbalance. Not all symptoms, in other words, need to be eliminated. They should, however, be viewed as clues to the animal's overall health status, to what treatment might be most helpful, and to how the animal is responding to treatment.

## So much to choose from

There are many modalities available to treat people and animals: herbs, Reiki, homeopathy, Chinese herbs and acupuncture, Tellington Touch, massage, chiropractic, zero balancing, nutraceuticals, flower essences, ear candles, herbs, vitamins, aroma therapy, prayer, craniosacral massage, crystals, color therapy, psychic healing, conventional drugs, rolfing, vitamins, and more.

Some modalities tend to have more superficial effects and merely ease the symptoms, while others are more likely to deeply affect the body/energy field and improve the overall health of the animal. I feel that homeopathy and Chinese medicine are most likely to be able to rebalance the energy system of the dog to increase longevity and quality of life, and even improve the health of future generations. ❧

# 21

# Dog Massage 101

*Just like humans, dogs derive
physical and emotional
benefits from massage. Learn how and why.*

Whether your dog qualifies as a field trial champion or a couch potato, he can derive benefits from massage. In fact, all our canine friends, including those with demanding jobs, those with a more leisurely life style, and those with chronic problems that hinder activity, can benefit from massage.

## What Is Canine Massage?

Massage is a hands-on manipulation of the muscles and other soft tissues with the intent of benefiting the animal. In other words, massage is touch with a purpose, and it yields many physical and emotional benefits.

Physically, massage stimulates circulation, enhances range of motion, relieves muscle spasms, and encourages a healthier coat. The positive effects on mental attitude and emotions are just as important. For example, massage promotes relaxation, reduces stress, fosters a sense of well-being, and strengthens the bond between human and animal.

Massage, which to the casual observer appears to range from gentle stroking to more vigorous kneading and percussion of tissues, affects the dog physically and emotionally by markedly influencing the nerve, muscle, circulatory, and lymph systems of the body.

*Some massage therapists incorporate acupressure or other thera-pies into their dog massage routines.*

In fact, none of the body's systems works in isolation. It is estimated that the human body has 60,000 miles of capillaries. Dogs have a pro-portionately similar amount, taking into consideration the size dif-ference between a Chihuahua and Great Dane. Each muscle fiber or cell is surrounded by three or four of these tiny blood vessels, which bring oxygen and nutrients to the cells and carry waste products away.

The nervous system communicates with each muscle cell through processes of the several million neurons (or nerve cells) which carry messages to the brain indicating whether the muscle is relaxed, con-tracted, or injured. Similarly, messages return to the muscles and stimulate them to respond by contracting or relaxing.

With this abundance of nerve and muscle cells and their associ-ated capillaries, it is not difficult to understand the impact that touch has on the body. The number of cells influenced by a single gentle stroke along the length of the body is mind-boggling.

Massage enhances circulation by stimulating the movement of blood through the capillaries which increases the supply of oxygen and nutrients to muscle cells and carries away waste products and toxins generated by contraction. Stimulation by massage enhances muscle tone. Tiny areas of muscle in spasm are encouraged to relax and the overall health of muscle and nerve are improved.

Also, massage relaxes your dog just as a massage or even a good shoulder and back rub relaxes your tight muscles when you are stressed. Massage also affects the capillaries that nourish the skin with oxygen and nutrients and cleanse it of wastes and toxins. This fosters a healthy skin and coat.

# The Mind/Muscle Connection

Your dog's body works just like yours. Daily use or lack of it can cause muscles to become tight, sore, stiff, or flaccid. Emotional stress can also affect your dog's muscles and general well-being. How does your dog react to potentially stressful situations like a trip to the vet, separation from you, or an encounter with a neighborhood dog? Like humans, part of a dog's response to stress may manifest as tense, tight muscles. Massage can go a long way to reverse the adverse results of stress-producing events by relaxing your dog, relieving his tension. It can also greatly enhance your bond with your dog.

We must keep in mind that the systems of the body work together as an integrated unit. Events—good or bad—that impact one system lead to a cascade of effects that eventually impact all systems.

---

...MASSAGE IS TOUCH WITH A PURPOSE

AND IT YIELDS MANY PHYSICAL AND

EMOTIONAL BENEFITS.

---

## A "whole body" dynamic

Consider, for example, what happens if your dog suffers a cut on one of his paws. Certainly there will be some loss of blood and infection-fighting white blood cells will rush to the area. The involvement of the circulatory system is obvious. Then the area surrounding the cut will swell with cellular fluids released due to the damage. Now the lymphatic system will swing into action to decrease the swelling by removing the excess fluid and carrying off other cellular debris resulting from the injury.

*Without regular hands-on massage sessions, this older, slightly arthritic dog develops tight, knotted muscles, and becomes cranky with pain.*

Because the dog's paw is sore, he may compensate for the pain by limping or shifting weight from one part of the body to another. This can stress healthy joints and muscles causing them to become misaligned and strained and to suffer abnormal wear and tear.

Needless to say, the pain will affect the dog, emotionally lowering his spirits and possibly his appetite.

Just as a minor cut can upset the body's balance and affect some aspect of virtually every system, massage can bring about positive changes to many systems of the body. An open wound should never be directly massaged. However, massage above or below an injury can stimulate blood flow which increases the supply of nutrients needed for repair and healing. Similarly, a stimulated lymph system hastens removal of wastes and excess fluids so swelling recedes.

# A Complement

Massage is not a substitute for conventional veterinary care but can often be very effectively used in conjunction with conventional care to provide maximum benefit to your dog. There are times when massage is contraindicated. As noted, one should never massage an open wound. Similarly, massage is contraindicated over surgical sites, insect bites, and skin infections. Massage is also inappropriate for an animal that has a temperature or swollen lymph glands, or cancer, is in a state of shock, or has a broken bone or ruptured disk. These conditions require conventional veterinary care.

Massage can benefit the rapidly growing muscles and mind of a puppy, the hard-working body of a canine athlete, and the chronic problems like hip dysplasia and arthritis common in older dogs. ❖

# 22

# Hot & Cold Weather Care

*Every season brings its own set of
concerns and cautions
for dog owners.*

Caring for our dogs is a year-round job, but our canine pals have different need and care requirements depending on the season. Summer brings warmth and longer days, but with that comes the risk of heatstroke, dehydration, ticks and fleas. Winter, with shorter daylit hours, requires extra caution when walking our pets at night, and extra care for their snow- and ice-exposed feet. Springtime is shedding time and in fall the days grow short and visibility becomes a concern.

Just as for humans, early summer is a great time for dogs. Getting out to play, especially after being cooped up for months is a joy. But balancing summer recreation with heat safety is serious business for dogs. As any critical care veterinarian will tell you, heatstroke is one of the summer's most frequent—and most lethal— canine afflictions.

## Sun Sense

Hershey, a 13-year-old black Chow belonging to Michael and Kristy Penno in Portsmouth, RI, loves to walk. For her owners, a primary challenge will be to help Hershey, in her full-length coat of fur, find ways to beat the heat.

Hershey's owners take many precautions to help her stay cool. On the advice of the experts, they strive to ensure adequate ventilation and shelter from the sun at all times. When the Pennos venture out in the summertime, they prefer to leave Hershey at home, restricting her outdoor activity to the cooler hours of morning and evening, after she has had ample time to digest her breakfast or dinner. This protects Hershey from the direct rays of the sun and also prevents burning her footpads on hot black asphalt, which absorbs enough heat to injure the extra thick flesh on her paws. She never walks on pavement that her owners would not cross in their own bare feet.

Her body, much closer to the ground than the bodies of her human counterparts, is also more vulnerable to the heat emanating from the road. Temperatures at two and three feet above the ground can be 20 degrees hotter than at six feet. Michael and Kristy also always pack a fresh supply of water and a collapsible bowl just the same.

While the family's acquisition of an air conditioner had little to do with Hershey, she usually prefers reaping its benefits to trudging along in the noontime sun on streets crowded with noisy traffic. Anyone who cares for a snub-nosed, or brachycephalic breed of dog, such as a Pekingese, pug, or English bulldog, should seriously consider the purchase of an indoor cooling system for the summer months. Due to a malformation of the soft palate, such dogs are less able to cool themselves by panting. They will actually exhaust themselves and worsen the situation with their panting; a condition called *ineffectual panter syndrome*.

# Sunburn Prevention

Hershey is a dark-skinned dog, so she is less vulnerable to the sun's rays than lighter-skinned dogs. With lighter skinned dogs, it is wiser to keep a longer coat for protection against the sun. Some dog owners even opt to have lightly pigmented areas tattooed or tinted with ink to make them less vulnerable to the sun's rays. For example, the pink rims of a white pit bull terrier's eyes are particularly susceptible to sunburn and could benefit from artificial pigmentation—a procedure performed only by a reliable veterinarian.

Dogs, too, can suffer serious sunburns. Hershey's owners avoid using sunblocks because she tends to lick them off of most areas of her body. Instead, they find that dressing her in a loose, white T-shirt or providing a source of shade such as a beach umbrella is more effective in blocking out the sun. Should Hershey suffer a burn, the Pennos would apply cool towels to the irritated skin and use an aloe vera preparation for its soothing effects. Most topical ointments, however, induce licking, which will further aggravate damaged skin.

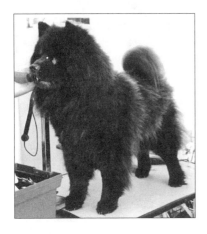

*Hershey, a 13-year-old Chow, before & after: She gets a lion cut each summer to help her stay cool.*

# Spring Grooming

Hershey's thick coat usually receives a complete professional groom-ing each spring, including the removal of her thick winter under-coat and a short lion cut. "In actuality," says Sally Geary, the grooming manager at Petsmart in Warwick, RI, "fur is not the prob-lem people think it is. It offers protection and insulation from the sun. For instance, for a Golden Retriever, I would recommend brush-ing or blowing out the winter hair rather than shaving it down."

For Hershey, the short coat cuts are invigorating. It also helps her owners to monitor her for ticks and fleas. Hershey's first cut of this season revealed a hot spot; a raw, irritated patch of skin that can be caused by many things, but which tends to fester under thick lay-ers of fur, especially with continued gnawing. Adequate ventilation in the form of fur removal is essential in the treatment of hot spots.

# The Danger of Heat Stroke

The worst case scenario for any dog is to suffer heat stroke. Certain dogs by virtue of heredity or life history may be particularly vul-nerable. Any pet that has a history of heat stroke will be more sus-ceptible, and you should make appropriate preventive measures. Hershey's owners make a routine of checking her normal vital signs, such as her heart rate, respiratory rate, rectal temperature and cap-illary refill time, so that they will recognize any significant aberra-tions. This will help them to know when immediate steps must be taken to restore Hershey's health in the event she suffers heat stroke.

Should this happen, her internal temperature would soar, possibly up to 110 degrees, causing irreversible brain damage and/or death. Her symptoms might include: elevated body temperature, vigorous panting, unsteady gait, physical depression or agitation, thick saliva or froth at the nose or mouth, rigid posture, muddy mucous membranes, (delayed capillary refill time) vomiting, bloody diarrhea, collapsing, and signs of shock.

# Treating Heat Stroke

Treating heat stroke involves cooling the dog from the inside out.

■ First, the dog should be removed from the source of heat to cooler surroundings, such as a room indoors, with a fan directed on his body, or the breezy shade of a tree.

■ Then the dog's entire body should be dampened with cool, (never cold) water, keeping in mind that when only the surface areas of the body are cooled, the superficial blood vessels restrict, forming an insulating layer that actually traps heat deeper inside the body. Ice packs should be restricted to the head, neck and chest.

■ While tempting the dog to drink cool water or to lick ice cubes, don't force him to consume water orally. In a state of shock, he could easily choke. Instead, concentrate on keeping the dog's immediate surroundings cool, monitor vital signs and contact a veterinarian as soon as possible. Heat stroke always requires immediate professional supervision.

# More Summer Hazards

## Lawn chemical safeguards

For dogs and people who've been hibernating to escape a cold winter, spring offers an irresistible invitation to frolic outdoors. But spring also signals the beginning of chemical warfare against lawn-wrecking bugs and weeds. When used as directed, lawn chemicals rarely cause acute poisoning, but scientists know little about the long-term effects of exposure to these chemicals. Help safeguard your pooch's long-term health by following these guidelines to minimize its exposure to lawn chemicals:

■ Store lawn-care chemicals away from your dog and carefully follow the manufacturer's directions when mixing and applying these chemicals. Remove any puddles or piles of chemicals on the lawn, driveway, or sidewalk.

■ Keep your dog off the lawn until the chemicals have thoroughly soaked in—24 hours for liquids, but longer for granules.

■ Make a list of the chemicals you or your lawn-care company apply to your lawn. Your veterinarian will want to know what chemicals your dog may have been exposed to if it becomes ill. And check with town or city officials to see what chemicals are applied to the public areas where you walk your dog.

■ Keep your dog on a leash or confined to your yard to prevent it from getting into your neighbor's chemical arsenal.

## Water hazards

During the sweltering dog days of summer, pooches sometimes plunge into swimming pools or ponds to beat the heat. Alas, drowning due to exhaustion can occur if a dog can't get out of a pool or a steeply banked natural body of water.

To avoid tragedy:

■ Don't let your dog run at large.

■ If you own a pool, install a secure fence around it and never let your dog wander inside the pool area unsupervised. Also, show your dog where the shallow-end steps are and how to use them.

In case of accident:

■ If the dog is unconscious, place the animal on an incline with its head tilted downward, pull its tongue forward, and gently push on its chest to help clear the airways of water.

■ Check for heartbeat and breathing. If either has stopped, initiate resuscitation while someone else drives the dog to the nearest veterinarian.

# Lifesaving Reminders

*It never ceases to appall the conscientious caregiver to see a dog locked inside of a car in the summer heat. This is a veritable death sentence, since the temperature inside of a baking car can soar to 160 degrees in a matter of minutes, even with the windows partially open. The sun's shifting makes parking in the shade unreliable. If it's uncomfortably hot for the driver, it's dangerous for a dog. Never hesitate to contact your local animal control officer through the police department if you suspect that immediate intervention is warranted. If a pet gets overheated:*

> ■ *Get him into shade and apply cool (not cold) water all over his body.*
> ■ *Apply ice packs or cold towels only to head, neck and chest.*
> ■ *Let him drink small amounts of cool water, or lick ice cubes or ice cream.*
> ■ *Get your pet to a veterinarian right away—it could save his life.*
> ■ *Remember, on hot days, your pet is safer at home!*

# Spring: Surviving Shedding Season

We all relish the warmer, longer days of spring. But increased daylight is a major trigger for the 4- to 5-week spring shedding season. "During the spring, hair follicles [the cavities out of which hair grows] that were resting all winter go through a growth spurt, and new hairs push out the old ones," explains Dr. Richard Anderson, staff veterinarian and dermatologist at Angell Memorial Animal Hospital in Boston.

Because shedding is a normal physiological process for most dogs (except for poodles, some wire-haired terriers, and a handful of other breeds that have continuously growing, humanlike hair), there's not much you can do about shedding other than help the process along. Start with a bath. "A vigorous bath with a good dog shampoo loosens up lots of dead hair," says Ms. Freddie Vecchi, a certified dog groomer at Dewberry's Dogs in Boston. Keep in mind that none of the "anti-shedding" potions available from pet-supply catalogs and stores have been clinically proven to reduce shedding. "It's bathing and grooming, rather than any active ingredient in a lotion or shampoo, that alleviates shedding," says Dr. Anderson.

If you're brave enough to tackle the bathing process at home, keep your dog's safety in mind. Place a towel or rubber mat in the bottom of the tub so your dog doesn't slip, and give your dog—and yourself—periodic "time outs" to rest.

After drying your dog, use a combination of tools (depending on what kind of coat your dog has) to remove more dead hair. The most popular utensil for brushing out long- and thick-coated dogs is the wire-pin slicker brush, and steel-tined grooming rakes are good for removing hair from dogs with densely packed undercoats. "But you should use rakes and slicker brushes with care because overzealous use can 'burn' your dog's skin," cautions Ms. Vecchi. If your dog has a middle-of-the-road coat like that of a golden or Labrador retriever, Ms. Vecchi recommends the nubbly rubber Zoom Groom™. "It removes hair effectively without the risk of hurting a dog's skin," says Ms. Vecchi.

Although fur will inevitably fly during shedding season, there are several ways to repel or remove dog hair from clothing and furniture. "I use antistatic spray on my car seats and clothes, which does a pretty good job of repelling hair," says Ms. Vecchi. You can also buy hair-pickup rollers and gloves, but a regular old lint brush or adhesive packing tape works just as well. With their large surface area, the adhesive backs of overnight-package airbill pouches also work wonders.

If shedding season puts you in surrender mode, "you could change your wardrobe, carpet, and furniture upholstery so it matches your dog's coat color," quips Dr. Anderson.

# Cold-Weather Cautions

## Chemicals and ice

Even in balmy climes, the mercury in fall and winter.. Here's how to dodge some outdoor wintertime dog hazards:

■ Antifreeze: Leaky car radiators can create a serious canine health risk—poisoning from sweet-tasting ethylene glycol, the main ingredient in most antifreeze. Thoroughly clean up antifreeze spills and store it in dog-proof containers. Use antifreeze containing the less-toxic ingredient propylene glycol.

■ Ice Balls: These painful paw-pad problems occur when cold snow crystallizes upon contact with warm, furry dog feet.Trim the hair between your dog's foot pads.If your dog develops "frozen feet," melt the ice balls with a warm, moist face cloth.

■ Road Salt: Many cities and towns treat icy streets and sidewalks with potentially irritating calcium salts. Wash your dog's paws after walking in areas treated with ice-melting compounds. Discourage your dog from chewing or licking his feet if he has walked through road salt and prevent his access to chemical deicers stored in your home.

## Walking in the dark

Along with crisp autumn air come earlier sunsets and later sunrises. This means your morning and evening dog walks may soon be shrouded in darkness. You can't rely on your pooch's tapetum lucidum (a layer in the canine eyeball that makes a dog's eyes shine with reflected light) to brighten your path. But there are several reliable ways to keep you and your pooch safe during your darkened forays:

■ Leash your dog and keep it close to your side at all times.

■ Using ID tags, tattoos, or microchips, make sure your dog can be easily identified for prompt return if, by chance, the two of you are separated.

■ Make sure you and your dog are highly visible.

■ Use passive-illumination devices such as reflective collars and vests for your dog and reflective footwear and clothing for yourself.

■ Consider battery-powered active illumination for greater protection. Devices range from hand-held or strapped-on lanterns to retractable leashes with flashlights built into the handle and flashing safety collars. Not only will these devices alert passing motorists, they will also announce your presence to other animals and possibly prevent unwanted encounters with wandering wildlife.

■ Prevent your dog from running at large in *all* seasons. ❧

# 23

# Clean Teeth —
# The First Defense

*Keeping your dog's teeth clean
is critical; here's how to
do it yourself.*

At some time or another, every dog lover has endured a blast of bad breath from an ardent canine companion. Foul-smelling breath is so prevalent among pooches that the very phrase has come to be an insult, as in, "Get lost, dog breath!"

Even so, a mention of the idea of preventive dental hygiene for dogs strikes some people as weird, if not nearly ridiculous. "Toothbrushes for dogs? You've got to be kidding!"

But it's no joke. Chew on these findings: a 1995 University of Minnesota epidemiology study of 67,000 dogs and cats showed oral disease to be the most common canine and feline clinical disease. And a 1996 Kansas State University study showed periodontal disease to be associated with chronic internal organ diseases of the heart, kidneys, and liver.

Our own dog husbandry practices are to blame for most of the factors that contribute to the poor condition of our dogs' choppers— including the diets that we provide for our dogs and human-engineered breeding programs.

Fortunately, this means that dog owners also have the power to reverse this unhealthy trend: You can observe your pooch's teeth for early signs of trouble, enabling you to treat small problems before they worsen; you can give your dogs nutritional support for healthy teeth and gums; and you can help keep their teeth clean. By implementing a thoughtful plan for dental health, you can help ensure your dog's teeth will contribute to his longevity and zest for life, not to mention, help make his doggie "kisses" fresher!

# Clean Teeth = Good Health

The focus of all dental care is the removal of plaque, which is composed of a mixture of oral bacteria, bacterial sugars, salivary proteins, and food and cellular debris, and dental calculus, or tartar, which is comprised of a mixture of mineralized concretions of salivary calcium and phosphate salts. The presence of plaque on the teeth can cause gum inflammation or "gingivitis," visible as a reddening of the tissue along the gum line. (Tartar does not directly cause gingivitis; rather, the calculus serves as a spot for plaque to collect and for bacteria to multiply.)

With dogs, "cavities" in the teeth are rare; it's gingivitis that wreaks havoc with the dog's health. Initially, it's the pain of gingivitis that diminishes the dog's quality of life; not only do dogs use their mouths for eating or drinking, but also for grooming, social interaction, and playing with toys. If a dog is reluctant to use his mouth for any of these activities, his gum problems can worsen due to reduced circulation.

If the gingivitis advances to a full-blown infection, it can make the dog very sick. "One single infected root can make a dog—or a person, for that matter—seriously ill," warns Dr. Nancy Scanlan, a veterinarian with a holistic practice in Sherman Oaks, California. "And oral infection can constantly enter your bloodstream and cause trouble elsewhere in the body. It can wreak havoc with the joints, lungs, kidneys, liver...you can get into multiple body problems from one little tooth."

# Man-made Problem

No one is likely to verify this first-hand, but wild canines like wolves and coyotes are unlikely to share domesticated dogs' dental problems, in large part because our dogs don't use their teeth in the same way as their wild brethren. The sharp front teeth of dogs are designed for cutting through tissue and tearing raw meat; the powerful jaws and sturdy back teeth are best used for gnawing on and crushing bones. Wild canines who engage in these activities daily generally have strong teeth that are scraped clean, with healthy gums.

But the efficient design of the dog's teeth is wasted on our domestic pets, who usually eat kibble or canned food. Dog teeth were never intended to chew foods like these. (Ironically, it's we humans, who have teeth that are ideally suited for chewing nuggets of dry dog food—grinding teeth with flattened tops.) Canned and soft food are even worse for dogs' teeth; they lack even the minimal abrasive action provided by dry food, and are more likely to contain sugars that contribute to dental disease.

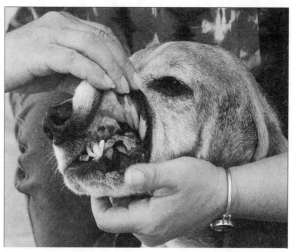

*This older dog displays the classic effects of long-term dental neglect: tartar-encrusted teeth and resultant gingivitis.*

Humans have also expedited their dogs' dental problems through hundreds of generations of breeding to create a tremendous variety in the shape and size of dogs, especially in the canine head. Unique characteristics have been refined in different breeds over time. Most dogs still have 42 permanent teeth, regardless of size or shape of the jaw. But in many breeds, this has resulted in crowding of teeth, which can lead to increased retention of plaque, gingivitis (inflammation of the gums), and eventually, to loss of teeth and infection. Today, tooth extractions are routine in a multitude of breeds; without extractions, many dogs would be unable to survive the crowded, dysfunctional mouths they have inherited.

# Teeth Cleaning Controversies

Everyone agrees that dogs' teeth should be clean. But as soon as we begin to talk about ways to remove plaque from our dogs' teeth, arguments ensue. The people who maintain that by feeding our dogs a diet that is as close to that of wild canines as possible (consisting largely of raw meat and bones), contend that dogs should be able to maintain clean teeth all on their own. Others say that feeding raw meat and bones is time-consuming, expensive, and potentially dangerous to the dog. Dogs can die from ingesting bacteria in raw meat and slivers from bones, they argue, and they are more than happy to brush their dogs' teeth, if that's what is necessary to keep their dogs "safe" from the pitfalls of the meat and bones diet.

One truth that stands above the fray is that you don't have to stand by helplessly while  sinister events are taking place in your dog's mouth. Obviously, there are advantages and disadvantages to every dental health approach. As always, you will have to choose the options that make the most sense for you and your dog.

# Regular Dental Exams

That said, be aware that most veterinarians maintain that the first part of a good dental health program is professional evaluation. An oral exam should be an integral part of every veterinary checkup, starting from a puppy's earliest health examination. Your veterinarian will check your puppy's bite to make sure the teeth mesh well, and to monitor the loosening of her deciduous (or "baby") teeth and the eruption of her permanent teeth.

Normally, in the process of shedding the deciduous teeth, the roots dissolve and the newly unmoored teeth fall out, in order to make way for the permanent teeth. When these baby teeth are said to be "retained," it's because the roots have failed to dissolve normally. If a tooth is erupting awry, or the deciduous teeth are retained, your veterinarian will be able to judge whether or not to intercede with an extraction, or whether some method of orthodontia should be used to bring errant teeth to the appropriate place.

As your dog ages, your veterinarian will also be able to monitor the condition of any teeth your dog may have broken or worn down to the nub. These conditions don't always require treatment, but they must be observed for signs of infection or other problems.

# Professional Cleaning

In addition to examinations, many veterinarians feel that dogs should have at least one annual prophylactic teeth cleaning to support all-around health—even though some dog owners have concerns about the anesthesia required for these procedures. In an effort to expose the dog to as few drugs as possible, as long as the examination showed that a dog's teeth were clean and white, some veterinarians would sanction passing up the annual cleaning.  But given the number of

*Brushing your dog's teeth takes practice, for you and your dog! With patience (and apparently with yummy dog toothpaste), 9-year-old Katherine convinced our test dog to comply.*

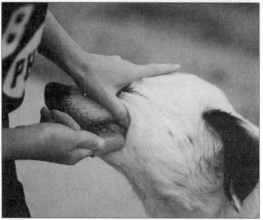

serious health concerns that bad teeth can cause, other veterinarians make a case for a more aggressively preventative plan.

According to Edward Eisner, DVM, Diplomate of the American Veterinary Dental College, "Ideally, a dog should have its teeth cleaned within the first 18 months of life. A perfect time to do this is while the dog is being anesthetized for spaying or neutering. Teeth cleaning visits should also include an educational session with the pet's owner, to teach toothbrushing."

During this initial educational visit, Eisner suggests that veterinarians gauge the owner's interest in home dental care. The suggested interval between teeth-cleaning visits, he says, will depend on the condition of the dog's mouth and the owner's interest in or ability to maintain the dog's clean teeth.

According to Dr. Eisner, a thorough cleaning will include ultrasonic scaling to remove plaque and calculus above and beneath the gumline, in addition to manual work with hand-held dental tools. Periodontal therapy, he says, goes a step beyond routine cleaning, by scaling the root surfaces. Finally, polishing the tooth surface is accomplished with a tiny, vibrating rubber cup and abrasive dentifrice to discourage plaque adherence.

One of the reasons these thorough cleanings are necessary, says Eisner, is because dogs with periodontal disease may or may not exhibit problems. Their owners may report nonclinical signs of tooth problems, without recognizing them as such. These behaviors include poor self-grooming, incessant nose licking, hesitancy to open or close the mouth all the way, decreased chewing of toys or treats, pawing at the mouth, facial rubbing, head or mouth handling shyness, or a sudden preference for soft food. Other symptoms include bad breath, sneezing, and one-sided nasal discharge.

Owners of small dogs and older dogs need to devote more time and attention to their dogs' teeth, says Eisner, because these dogs have a much higher incidence of periodontal disease than do large or young dogs. "In a situation of chronic inflammation, the bone will shrink away from the gums at a rate of 1.5 mm per year. An Akita tooth may have a root 30 mm thick, a Chihuahua only 5 mm thick. At the rate of 1.5 mm per year of bone loss, the Akita has time before there is a noticeable problem, but the Chihuahua has only a couple of years before radical therapy is needed," Eisner says.

# The "Ancestral" Diet

There are dog-care experts who feel that brushing and cleaning a dog's teeth is completely unnecessary if the dog is fed a diet similar to that of his wild ancestors. One of the most well-known advocates of this approach is Dr. Ian Billinghurst, an Australian veterinarian and author of *Give Your Dog a Bone*, published in 1993. Billinghurst says that a diet of raw foods, particularly bones and meats, stimulate health in the whole animal in every way, but particularly for oral health. Billinghurst states in his book, "Prior to recommending bones as an essential part of a dog's diet, I had to deal with masses of revolting, stinking, disease-ridden mouths, just like every other vet. Gradually, as my clients took my advice and fed their dogs bones, that unpleasant job was on the wane."

Due to the vocal advocacy of holistic breeders and veterinarians like Billinghurst, the number of people who feed their dogs only meaty bones and other raw foods is increasing. Yet most conventionally trained veterinarians are still warning their clients about the dangers of such a diet. They tell horror stories about dogs with bones stuck in their throats and dogs with intestinal impactions caused by bone consumption.

"The jury is still out among conventional veterinarians, mainly due to the problems...associated with a dog eating too many, or the wrong kinds of bones," comments veterinary homeopath and nutritionist Dr. Jan Facinelli, of Denver, Colorado. "However, dogs can learn to handle raw foods and bones, especially if they are started young, in controlled situations. I see a number of dogs who eat only raw and home-cooked foods, and, generally, they are very healthy animals. There's something about fresh foods  that contributes to good nutrition—and good nutrition supports healthy gums and teeth."

Dr. Facinelli recommends that her clients feed their dogs large knuckle bones with cartilage on the joints as a good chewing source with teeth cleaning benefits.

Other holistic practitioners feel that if a dog's diet is truly healthy, and he has plenty of opportunities to exercise his teeth and gums, he should not require any routine dental cleaning. Facinelli, however, feels there's no substitute for occasional toothbrushing. "The benefits of brushing the dog's teeth are huge, even if it's just once every two weeks," she says. "Plus, it takes just five minutes, and is well worth the effort."

# Chew Toys

Necessity is the mother of marketing; as a result, there are literally thousands of products advertised as beneficial to dogs' dental health. And there are also thousands of opinions about the dangers or virtues of each of these products.

Rope-based toys have gained popularity as "dog dental floss," and there are dozens of toys that incorporate knotted ropes into their designs: mint-scented ropes, ones that "crackle," ropes with plastic pieces that are meant to be chewed, and so on. As consumption of these products increases, increasing numbers of veterinarians are extracting rope and string from various parts of their patients' anatomy.

The same can be said of every other type of toy; most veterinarians have performed surgery on at least a few dogs with hunks of Nylabone, rawhide, Frisbee, or other toy materials impacted in their intestines.

## Recommendations

We asked Eisner to help us formulate chew-toy recommendations.

■ His first caution is to use simple common sense: watch your dog when he's chewing on anything. "Each dog is different, and can be judged on a continuum, from irrational chewers to speculative ones," Eisner laughs. Just because a dog has never chewed up or swallowed one toy is no guarantee that he won't ingest the next one you give him, says Eisner. "Supervision is required any time you give your dog something to put in his mouth."

■ Next, Eisner recommends choosing chews which either soften as the dog chews them, or products that "give," but do not readily crack or split. One such toy is the Dental Kong, described by Eisner as, "a terrific device, made of non-harmful materials, and resilient."

What about rawhide chews, or animal products, such as pig ears? "There is dental benefit to rawhide, but it's critical that you keep an eye out for little pieces coming off and being swallowed," Eisner said. "When rawhide toys get soft enough to start coming apart, they must be taken from the dog."

There has been much debate about the dangers of the preservatives and other chemicals present in rawhide. Holistic veterinarian Dr. Facinelli feels the benefits of rawhide as an oral cleaning device outweigh their chemical dangers. "You can't be too rigid," says Facinelli. "Of course you should limit your dog's intake of additives, but look at the benefits of achieving a clean mouth!"

Eisner gives slower approval, and a stronger warning, to the concept of raw (never cooked) bones used as a dental cleaning agent. "Of course, raw bones can get the job done, but you must supervise your dog as a safeguard against the bone splintering and subsequent slivering. Without supervision, dogs can easily end up swallowing sharp pointy objects that may injure the delicate lining of the digestive tract," he warns.

# Delivering the Goods

All of these substances are available in several delivery systems: toothpastes (which are generally scrubbed onto the teeth and gums), gels (topically applied to the gums), liquid rinses (which are squirt-

*Test differ-
ent brushes
to find the
one that
works best
for you.*

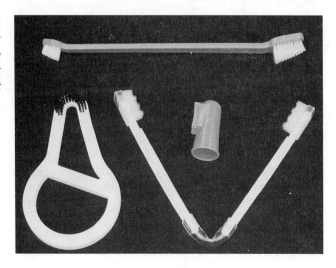

ed into the mouth), rawhide chews that have been impregnated with the substances, and small cloth pads (which are wiped onto the teeth and gums). In Eisner's estimation, the most effective are the tooth-pastes and the rawhide chews, because of the abrasive action they provide; the least helpful are the pads.

"If you think about your own teeth-cleaning experiences, it's easy to judge these different forms," he says. "The goal is to apply the dentifrice to as many surfaces of the teeth and gums as possible. One benefit of the liquids is that they readily wash into crevices and crannies in the dog's teeth and gums. But a shortcoming is that they provide no abrasive or scrubbing action; imagine only using mouth-wash, and never brushing your teeth."

Eisner finds the teeth-cleaning pads to be the least useful deliv-ery system, since they can neither deliver the dentifrices to every surface of the dog's teeth or gums, nor scrub the teeth very efficiently.

# Council for Further Study

If a group of veterinarians who are dedicated to dentistry are able to form a consensus opinion better than the rest of the canine com-munity, picking the best dental-health products for our dogs will soon be much easier! Recently, a number of interested veterinari-ans formed a group that is devoted to providing an objective, cred-ible means of identifying veterinary dental products that are effective in controlling accumulation of plaque and tartar. Members of the group, the Veterinary Oral Health Council (VOHC), were concerned about the advertising "noise" in the marketplace, especially in the absence of any objective means of recognizing efficacious products.

"The VOHC is a new regulatory body that will function in a fashion parallel to the American Dental Association, endorsing products with a seal of acceptance for veterinary use," Eisner describes. Based on the results of tests devised (but not conducted) by the Council, they will award a seal of approval for products that are shown to help control plaque and/or help control tartar. This Council should also attract the involvement of the veterinarians who have special interests in dentistry, and provide a concentrated source of information about developments in the field for interested dog owners—and journalists!

# D-I-Y Teeth Cleaning

While occasional professional cleaning is important, toothbrushing is the best way to remove plaque from the dog's teeth. Any soft-bristled toothbrush may be used—it doesn't have to be a special brush for dogs, although several manufacturers have innovated brushes that can make the task marginally easier.

■ Nylabone, for instance, makes a handy two-sided brush that allows you to scrub both sides of a tooth at the same time.

■ The bristles of Crazy Dog's "Easy Grip PetAdent" are arranged in a semicircle, for the same purpose.

■ The PetAdent's bristles are black, reportedly because they are easier to see against white teeth.

■ Several manufacturers also make rubber or plastic "fingertip" brushes that you slip on like finger of a glove; they have bristles affixed to the tip.

■ Four Paws Products makes a long-handled brush with a large head at one end and a small head at the other—great for long-nosed dogs and big dogs.

## Not Recommended

There is one toothbrushing product on the market that Dr. Eisner is vigorously opposed to: the Plaque Whacker.

The cleaning brush on this device resembles the scrubbing material that kitchen sponges are sometimes backed with, only it's much stiffer. This device is brutal against delicate oral tissues and the thin enamel of dogs' teeth. It can also cause microscopic etch marks on the teeth, creating sites for plaque adhesion.

# The Value of Toothpaste

Toothpaste is not necessary to get the dog's teeth clean, though it can make the project easier. Don't use the stuff from your family's medicine cabinet, however. Special meat- or peanut butter-flavored toothpastes for dogs have two advantages: they are far more attractive to dogs than minty "people" toothpastes, and they contain substances that are better suited to killing the bacteria found in dog mouths.

Toothpastes can work two ways: mechanically and chemically. Some contain inert abrasive materials such as calcium or silicate, which take a significant mechanical role in helping scrub plaque and other matter from the teeth and gums. But even those pastes without abrasives can play a mechanical role, by lubricating the bristles of a toothbrush for better action.

Toothpastes can also work chemically. Today, a variety of substances are employed to kill the bacteria that lends itself to plaque formation. Two such substances are chlorhexidine and hypothiocyanate. The former kills the aerobic (oxygen-dependent) bacteria commonly found in a healthy dog mouth. The latter is aimed at killing the pathogenic (illness-causing) anaerobic bacteria that multiply in and "infect" periodontal pockets in an unhealthy dog mouth. Which type of product you use should depend on the condition of your dog's periodontal area (the gum/tooth margin). If the dog has tight, pink gums and teeth with little tartar, the chlorhexidine products are more appropriate. The hypothiocyanate products are helpful when the dog is known to have periodontal problems.

# Diet and Dental Health

From your dog's dental-health perspective, anything that mechanically removes plaque—the sticky accumulation of bacteria, food particles, and saliva on teeth that precedes more serious dental disorders—is helpful. Thus, it's generally believed that eating dry dog food reduces the risk of gingivitis (gum inflammation) and periodontitis (severe inflammation and erosion of tissue surrounding the teeth).

But when it comes to attacking plaque, dry food can't hold a candle to regular tooth brushing. "If you brush your dog's teeth every day or two, it doesn't really matter what it eats," notes Dr. Cecilia Gorrel, a veterinary dentist practicing in the U.K. Also, when brushing your dog's teeth, you're more likely to notice other oral anomalies, such as tooth fractures or early-stage tumors.

While hard, abrasive kibble can help clean your dog's teeth, "for dry food to effectively scrape the teeth, the dog has to chew the food, not swallow it whole," notes Dr. Laura LeVan, clinical assistant professor at Tufts University School of Veterinary Medicine. Consequently, the size of the kibble and your dog's eating style will help determine dry food's plaque-removal power. Also be wary of teeth-cleaning claims made by manufacturers of crunchy dog treats. To get dental benefits from some of these, your dog may have to eat more of them than is healthy.

---

...THE MOST EFFECTIVE ARE THE

TOOTHPASTES AND THE RAWHIDE CHEWS,

BECAUSE OF THE ABRASIVE ACTION

THEY PROVIDE.

---

Unfortunately, even if you brush Bowser's teeth daily and feed him only dry food that he chews thoroughly, he may still develop tooth and gum problems. That's because the canine immune response to the bacteria in plaque varies dramatically from dog to dog. "I have seen dogs with massive plaque and tartar buildup and no periodontal disease and those with spotlessly clean mouths and severe periodontal disease," says Dr. Peter Kertesz, a dentist in the U.K. who also treats companion and zoo animals. Also, as a dog ages, its immune system weakens, making it more susceptible to the effects of periodontal bacteria.

While studies suggest that large dogs are less prone to periodontal disease than small dogs, individual genetic makeup largely determines a dog's susceptibility to the bacteria in plaque. So generalizations about size and breed may be misleading. Assuming a dog receives appropriate dental care, perhaps the best indicator of its prospects for "good teeth" is the oral health of its parents. ❧

# 24

# Putting Out the Fire

*Preventing—and dealing with—*
*your dog's painful and itchy "hot spots."*

O ne morning many years ago, I leaned over to stroke my
dog Mandy's luxurious black coat—and gasped. There was
an angry, oozing sore the size of a grapefruit on the outside of her right hind leg. It was cherry red, inflamed, and
looked incredibly painful. And I was horrified, because I worked at
a humane society at the time, and this looked like the kind of wound
for which we would investigate an irresponsible owner—irresponsible for not providing proper care and attention! I was sure it had-
n't been there the night before. What had happened to my dog? I
rushed her to my veterinarian.

Mandy had a "hot spot," due to, according to my vet, a flea allergy. Even when my veterinarian assured me that it didn't mean she
was infested with fleas, and that a single flea can trigger an allergic
reaction in a flea-sensitive dog, I still felt as if I had neglected her.

We treated the wound and it healed without complication. I tried
to improve my flea-control methods, and Mandy never had a recurrence of the ugly condition. But it's not always so easy to win
the hot-spot battle.

## What Is a Hot Spot?

A hot spot, according to Terry G. Spencer, DVM, of the Animal Health
Center in Salinas, CA, is known formally as "acute moist pyoderma,"

and is a signal of an underlying skin disorder. The most common disorder is a flea allergy, but hot spots are also linked to other conditions such as food allergies, poor nutrition, and thyroid disease.

Acute moist pyoderma is caused by the microorganism Staphylococcus intermedius. The organism is commonly found on the skin, and opportunistically takes advantage when the integrity of the skin is compromised by some underlying disorder. The skin is an organ whose vitally important function is to form a protective covering for the rest of the body, preventing the entry of foreign organisms that can infect and destroy the other organ systems. It's our dog's primary armor against any kind of bad bug. (And ours!)

When the staph. organism invades the skin at a weakened point (such as a flea bite in an allergic dog), it produces endotoxins that are destructive to skin cells. The body's immune system kicks into high gear, sending an army of mast cells, histamines, and other defensive bodies to the site of the hot spot. As the ensuing battle rages, the damage spreads, killing and consuming the skin in the process. The red, angry appearance of a hot spot is not simply a sign of irritated skin. The skin is actually gone.

"A hot spot is a critical medical emergency similar to the skin loss of a burn victim," says Dr. Spencer. "It can occur within a few hours, is intensely itchy and painful, and can progress to life-threatening if not treated. I have seen lesions grow from the size of a quarter to baseball-size within hours, and I have seen dogs with their entire sides sloughed away by this condition."

Dr. Spencer received her degree in veterinary medicine from Colorado State University in 1995, and worked at several California veterinary clinics prior to opening her Animal Health Center in 1998. She utilizes veterinary orthopedic manipulation, works closely with a human chiropractor who is certified in veterinary chiropractic, and is in training to receive her veterinary acupuncture certificate. She routinely integrates complementary modalities into her treatment protocols and is a firm believer in the holistic approach to veterinary care. Despite her strong interest and belief in complementary medicines, she treats hot spots traditionally because of the severity of the condition. Once the crisis is resolved she then uses a more natural approach to prevent further hot spots.

# Traditional Treatment

The standard veterinary treatment, according to Dr. Spencer, starts with clipping the hair around the affected area. The staph. organ-

*In addition to being unsightly and very painful, hot spots are an indication that the dog's immune system is failing to protect the dog adequately from bacteria.*

ism is characterized by an oozing serum that congeals and mats the surrounding fur. Clipping makes it easier to treat the wound and keep it clean. Then the area is scrubbed with a disinfectant.

"It is important," she cautions, "to use a disinfectant that is antiseptic (to kill the staph. and any other invading organism) but not caustic. I usually sedate the dog for this procedure because the hot spot is so intensely painful. Then I scrub with Chlorhexaderm or Betadine. Products like alcohol and peroxide must be avoided at all costs—they are extremely painful to an already excruciating wound, and peroxide will cause even more damage to the skin." After scrubbing the area, Dr. Spencer recommends application of a topical antiseptic/steroid spray such as Dermacool or Gentocin spray.

"It is critically important to halt the progression of damage as quickly as possible," she says. "Until we kill the staph. organisms and calm the hyper-reacting immune system the skin will continue to be eaten away. You can use a more natural approach with an oatmeal spray, but you run the risk of letting the infection get out of control. I prefer to use emergency measures to halt the damage. Then I'll talk to the client about how to improve the overall health of the dog holistically in order to minimize the chance of recurrence."

# The Cortisone Controversy

There is no question that steroids can do nasty things to our canine friends. Dogs are very sensitive to steroids. The powerful drug suppresses the immune system, which leaves the patient vulnerable to other problems that run the continuum from mild to serious—from a simple bladder infection to the potential for onset of diabetes.

Use of steroids can also be damaging to the adrenal system. Adrenal glands secrete steroids, and when these are administered medically it sends a signal to the adrenal glands to stop production. This can sometimes totally shut down the body's production of steroids. Steroids also cause our dogs to pant more, drink more, urinate and eat more, and can cause subsequent problems with incontinence and weight gain.

Dr. Spencer thinks steroids are a good thing to avoid unless they are absolutely necessary. In her opinion, hot spots make the use of steroids absolutely necessary.

"I do use steroids topically for hot spots, and I may give one injection of a short-acting steroid for stubborn cases, but," she adds, "I don't give oral steroids. If an owner doesn't give all the pills and keeps them in the cupboard, she may be too tempted to pop a few into her dog's mouth the next time he's a little itchy. This is a good way to get into trouble with steroids."

Other holistic practitioners we queried were less enthusiastic — and even rather condemning—about even sparing use of steroids for hot spots. Steroids do effect quick healing, but at a cost; they act in a suppressive manner, rather than supporting the body's homeostasis, or natural return to balance.

# Holistic Prevention

Once she has resolved the emergency through aggressive intervention, Dr. Spencer reverts to her holistic bias.

"The hot spot is just a symptom of an greater, underlying problem," she reiterates. "Flea hypersensitivity is the most common cause, but there are others. Contact dermatitis can cause the condition. For example, people think tea tree oil is good for skin problems, but some dogs are highly allergic to it. I have seen a number of hot spots caused by contact with strong concentrations of tea tree oil. Also, many dogs are allergic to the cedar chips that are contained in some dog beds. Generalized allergies—food, pollens, anything that compromises the skin and the immune system—can provide the environment for the staph. organism to take hold. The constantly 'itchy dog' is the most likely victim for recurring hot spots."

Dr. Spencer's answers to the prevention question are simple: Use good flea control. Provide excellent nutrition. Identify allergens and reduce exposure. Maintain good grooming practices. Look for (and treat) signs of anything that might be suppressing the immune system, such as low thyroid. Do everything you would otherwise do to keep your dog in the peak of health. Healthy dogs are not likely to suffer from hot spots.

Flea sensitivity truly is the number one cause of hot spots. Regular flea combing, vacuuming, diatomaceous earth, and nematodes are just some of the non-toxic, natural methods available for controlling those pesky bloodsuckers that can send out an open invitation for a staph. invasion.

Good nutrition not only aids in effective flea control, it also strengthens the body's immune system, reducing the likelihood of allergy problems. The Omega 6 and Omega 3 fatty acids, given in the proper ratio (5:1), have been shown to fight inflammation and to help promote healthy skin. Speaking of healthy skin and coat, keeping your dog well-groomed—no oily, dirty skin—will also help stave off the staph.

Overvaccination is now suspect in canine skin allergies as well, so you might want to talk to your veterinarian about revisiting your dog's vaccine schedule with an eye toward reducing the number of booster shots she gets. And, just like it does for us, exercise contributes to our dogs' overall good heath and condition. If your pooch is a couch potato, it might behoove both of you to add a 20 to 30-minute aerobic hike up the hill to your daily routine.

The holistic philosophy says that organisms function as complete units that cannot be reduced to the sum of their parts. If your dog gets a hot spot, by all means treat the "part," but then be sure to look beyond the immediate emergency to find the source of the problem. With hot spots, as with so many other health issues, if the complete unit is healthy it follows that the parts will also be healthy.

## Holistic Help For Hot Spots

*Some skin problems are caused by specific deficiencies, including vitamins A, E, C, or zinc. For any dog with skin problems, we suggest using a daily multiple vitamin and mineral supplement, and additional vitamin C.*

*A thorough but simple discussion of how food allergies can trigger hot spots can be found in Dr. Donald R. Strombeck's 1999 book,* Home-Prepared Dog and Cat Diets, *along with a number of Dr. Strombeck's suggested diets for allergic dogs.*

*Grapefruit seed extract, found in most health food stores, is an effective antibacterial agent. Dilute the 33 percent extract in five to six parts water and spray directly on hot spots. The unpleasant taste of grapefruit seed extract is helpful to discourage a dog from further licking and chewing of the hot spot.*

*Diluted half and half with water, apple cider vinegar can be sprayed on hot spots and the surrounding area to discourage bacteria growth, soothe the skin, and repel fleas and ticks.*

*In her book,* The Encyclopedia of Natural Pet Care, *herbal expert CJ Puotinen recommends making a 15 percent solution of tea tree oil for use on hot spots as an all-purpose disinfectant.*

*Puotinen recommends thoroughly mixing two tablespoons of tea tree oil with four tablespoons of 80-proof vodka, vegetable glycerin, or sulfated castor oil, and then adding either pure water, pure aloe vera juice, or comfrey or calendula tea to make a total of 3/4 cup of solution. This 15 percent tea tree oil solution can be sprayed on a hot spot, and also used on any surface where a safe disinfectant is needed.*

*Also, because some dogs have displayed sensitivity to tea tree oil, you should apply only a very small amount of this diluted formula the very first time you use it. Wait at least three to four hours before applying more, and discontinue use if the hot spot worsens. However, in our experience, most problems with tea tree oil are due to use of full-strength preparations.*

*Practitioners of Traditional Chinese Medicine (TCM) would explain that hot spots are areas of "stagnant heat" that have risen to the surface of the body. In her book,*

*Four Paws, Five Directions, veterinarian and TCM practitioner Dr. Cheryl Schwartz, of San Francisco, California, suggests using acupressure to clear the heat and dampness of hot spots and encourage circulation. Specifically, Dr. Schwartz suggests using acupressure behind the ears at Gall Bladder 20, or in front of the shoulders at Governing Vessel 14, Large Intestine 11 at the elbows, and Urinary Bladder 40 behind the knees.*

*To find the acupressure points shown here, palpate the area indicated. If you go slowly and don't push too hard, you'll find soft or hollow areas or areas where your fingers just want to stop; this is an acupressure point.*

*Once you locate an acupressure point, hold the flat pads of your fingers on the general area and press down slowly. Once you find a depth of pressure your dog is completely comfortable with, remain still for 30 to 60 seconds to allow him to adjust to your touch. Then begin to move the skin and tissues below the surface around in slow, deep circles.*

*Plant your fingers as you circle; do not slide over the hair. If your dog holds his breath, fusses, or moves away from you, reduce your pressure and just hold gently on the point. Resume the circles once he relaxes. Massage the point for one to three minutes, alternating between simply holding the steady pressure and circling.* 🐾

# 25

# Repelling Fleas

*Fleas are every dog's—and every owner's—
nightmare. But you don't have to resort to
chemical warfare to fight them.*

Every dog owner knows that getting rid of fleas can be one of the biggest challenges of dog-keeping. Few people know, however, that the process can also be the most damaging to their dog's health. Specifically, the use of insecticides on the dog and all around the dog's environment can cause nerve and liver damage, impair the immune system, and even cause cancer. And you have to wonder—if these effects have been noted in dogs, what effects do all these toxins have on the people who live with the dogs?

It's a real problem, because if you have fleas in your home, you have to do something. They can make your dog (and you and your family) miserable through their tiny but painful bites, as well as the allergic reactions that many people and dogs develop to flea saliva. They are prolific, producing thousands of eggs during their three- to four-month life-span. In ideal conditions the cycle takes just two weeks, from egg-laying to larvae to pupae to hatched fleas capable of laying eggs of their own.

## Toxic Families

There are a few major types of chemicals most widely used in the war on fleas: Organophosphates, most of which are readily absorbed through skin, eyes, stomach, and lungs, are among the most common pet insecticides and are responsible for the majority of pet poisonings.

Initially, overexposure can result in salivation, involuntary defecation, urination, and vomiting. This can progress to ataxia (lack of balance), convulsions, teary eyes, slow heartbeat, and labored breathing.

Carbamates are the second-most common compound in flea-control products. The effects of exposure to carbamates are generally less severe than organophosphates, and carbamates do not accumulate in the tissues. Dogs who are overexposed to carbamates will exhibit many of the same symptoms of poisoning as the organophosphate-poisoned dogs. Long-term, the chemicals can cause lowered production of bone marrow and degeneration of the brain.

Organochlorines, a third major class of insecticides, are not as immediately toxic as the first two, but do accumulate in the tissues and persist in the environment for years. (DDT, an organochlorine, was banned in 1972 but is still found in 55 percent of Americans.) Poisoning with this chemical may stimulate the dog to exhibit exaggerated responses to light, touch, and sound. Spasms or tremors can progress to seizures and death.

Yet another class of flea-killing chemicals, pyrethrins, are often labeled as "natural," due to the source of the poison: the chrysanthemum flower. But despite their origins, pyrethrins are still potentially dangerous, and have caused allergic dermatitis as well as systemic allergic reactions, vomiting, headaches and other nervous system disturbances.

# How Toxic Are These Pesticides?

An estimated 20,000 people receive emergency care annually for actual or suspected pesticide poisoning, and approximately 10 percent of these are admitted to the hospital. Each year, 20-40 people die of acute pesticide poisoning in the U.S.; most episodes of acute occupational poisoning are due to organophosphate and carbamate insecticide exposure. There are no numbers for animal poisonings.

Each of the chemicals mentioned above are intended to kill fleas via direct contact. In recent years, the focus of development of flea-killing chemicals has been on substances that affect only the fleas that actually bite a treated dog. These substances, which are either applied to or fed to a dog, are intended to linger in the dog's body without affecting his own chemistry, waiting to deliver a fatal blow to any flea that drinks his blood. While these chemicals are proving to be far less harmful than the older flea-killing substances, and conventional veterinarians enthusiastically encourage their use, many holistic practitioners are less enthusiastic about the drugs.

# Natural Flea Control

Fortunately, there are many natural, effective methods of controlling fleas widely recommended by both conventional and holistic veterinarians. The most successful approach will utilize several indoor and outdoor methods. A pesticide-free battle takes a little more time to win than one that utilizes deadly foggers and shampoos, but it has the advantage of not killing your dog.

Regular flea-combing is the most direct and low-tech method, and it works as a good flea-population monitor, too. Pet supply stores sell the fine-toothed combs that pull fleas through the fur and trap them. The comb is then dipped in warm soapy water to remove and kill the fleas.

Since fleas spend only a portion of their time on the dog, and eggs, larvae and pupae, are likely to be found in any area where the dog lives, most of your flea-eradication efforts should concentrate on your home and yard. This may not be welcome news, but the safest way to get rid of fleas is through fastidious housekeeping.

The length of the flea's life depends on environmental conditions, but it can live out its entire cycle in as little as three weeks or as

*It's easier to rid your house of fleas if your dog never leaves his yard, and there's no interaction with other cats and dogs. But if you take your dog out you're bound to bring new fleas home. That's why your natural flea-fighting project must be year-round.*

much as six months. Female fleas are prolific, laying as many as 20 to 50 eggs per day for as much as three months. Development of the larvae that hatch out of the eggs takes place off the dog, usually on or near the dog's bedding and resting areas, so concentrating on removing opportunities for the eggs to develop is the most effective population control strategy.

One way to remove the eggs' opportunities to develop is to remove the eggs, and to this end, your vacuum will be one of your most valuable tools in the flea war. Vacuum all the areas that your pet uses frequently, at least every two to three days. Since fleas locate their hosts by tracing the vibration caused by footsteps, vacuuming the most highly-trafficked hallways and paths in your house will be rewarding. Don't forget to vacuum underneath cushions on the couches or chairs your dog sleeps on. Change vacuum bags frequently, and seal the bag's contents safely in a plastic bag before disposing. Some people place flea collars in their vacuum bags, to kill any fleas or flea larvae they vacuum up; this is probably the safest application for the toxic plastics.

---

A PESTICIDE-FREE BATTLE ... HAS THE

ADVANTAGE OF NOT KILLING YOUR DOG.

---

# Get With the "Program"?

When the newest generation of flea-fighting chemicals arrived on the scene, veterinarians and dog owners rejoiced. Researchers had finally developed products that could be administered quickly, safely, and easily, and that didn't need to be reapplied every few days. Toxic baths, dips, sprays, collars, and powders could be thrown out.

Taking their place were two types of products. One was a type of chemical called an insect growth regulator, or, in layman's terms, "flea birth control." The most successful of these was lufenuron, marketed as "Program," introduced by Ciba-Geigy Corp. of Greensboro, NC, in 1992. Program is administered orally, in tablet form, once a month. Ingested by female fleas and deposited in her eggs, the drug interferes with the development of the eggs so they cannot hatch.

The biggest benefit of the drug: neither the dog nor its keepers are exposed to any toxic chemicals, and the life cycle of the flea is ended. But because the drug doesn't kill adult fleas, a dog could be bitten again and again by the adult fleas in his environment before they die of old age! And any new fleas that came on the scene via other dogs, or trips to infested areas, could also plague the dog.

## A little goes a long way

The other revolutionary new products are externally applied fat-soluble products. Only a small amount of the liquid is used, but it is wildly toxic to fleas. The fluid dissolves in the oils of the dog's skin, and spread in a micro-thin coating over his body. Depending on the dog, the chemicals are effective for 30 to 90 days. The first chemical is called fipronil, and is marketed under the name "Frontline" by Rhone Merieux. The second is imidacloprid, marketed by Bayer Corporation as "Advantage." The makers of both products claim that the chemicals are not absorbed into the bloodstream and internal organs.

Most conventional veterinarians are avid promoters of the drugs. The perspective of Joan Freed, DVM, a traditional practitioner and veterinary chief of staff for the Humane Society of Santa Clara Valley, in Santa Clara, California, is typical of most conventional veterinarians. She applauds the use of Frontline and Advantage, especially because they rendered the older generation of highly toxic chemicals commonly used for flea control obsolete.

"The new products are revolutionizing veterinary medicine," Freed says. "So much of veterinary treatment is flea-related—from deworming for tapeworms to treating the endless cases of flea allergy dermatitis. Advantage and Frontline appear to be highly effective, and very safe."

(Note that all three drugs are available only through veterinarians, and are typically marked up in price by as much as 200 percent or more. This in itself can lend impetus to veterinary enthusiasm.)

## Holistic practitioners take exception

The excitement about the chemicals is not common in the holistic veterinary community, however. When queried, we found the majority of veterinary practitioners who use alternative and natural modalities don't advocate the use of Advantage and Frontline, though the veterinarians were evenly split on the topic of Program.

"Advantage and Frontline are convenience pesticides, and everybody likes them because they don't have to mess around with a lot of other things," says Ihor Basko, a holistic veterinarian from Kapaa, Hawaii. "But the chemicals are not as safe as they are made to seem.

I've seen several dogs react to them, and some of my clients' cats have died after using them. Just read the label—it can cause eye irritation, it says not to get it on your skin or clothing, to wash your hands after handling it—and yet they say it's safe for your pet!" Fewer problems with Program

Dr. Basko is one of the practitioners who has no issues with Program, saying he hasn't seen any adverse effects from its use.

Dr. Christina Chambreau, of Baltimore, Maryland, is not among Program's fans but admits she would use it on an animal long before she would resort to Advantage or Frontline.

"I've heard of and seen some pretty severe problems with all of them," says the veterinary homeopath. "On several occasions, via email, I've asked a list of about 15 holistic veterinarians whether they have seen problems with these compounds, and the answer is always, 'Yes.'"

Even Chambreau has to admit that the substances are highly effective at ridding a dog and his home of fleas, and admits that she would never say they should never be used. "A lot of dogs are not bothered by these drugs, just like a lot of animals are not bothered by vaccines," she says. "But those that are bothered can have horrible reactions."

If a dog's only health problem was a flea allergy, chances are you'd improve his situation by using the substances, Chambreau says. But you'd be taking an unnecessary risk if you were to use them on a dog who had demonstrated sensitivity to other chemicals, or one that had cancer, autoimmune problems, or liver problems.

"You have to take something like this on a case by case basis," says Dr. Chambreau. "Even though the makers say it doesn't go through the liver, I've seen dogs with liver problems after being treated with it. So I'd try all the natural flea control methods first. If they all failed to diminish the flea problem, and the dog was fairly healthy otherwise, then I might be tempted to use Advantage or Frontline as a one-time deal, to try to break the fleas' life cycle in that home. And I must say I would use them before using their toxic predecessors."

# The Dirt on Dust

Some people use diatomaceous earth (also known as DE or Diatom Dust), a non-toxic powder more commonly used in swimming pool filters and as a garden soil amendment (the latter kind is the form used against fleas). The powder acts as a powerful desiccant on the waxy coating that covers fleas, technically dehydrating them to death.

It also kills flea larvae. DE can be sprinkled onto carpets and swept across wood floors (so it works into the cracks in the wood).

A couple of cautions: because it consists of tiny, hard particles, it can contribute significantly to wearing down your carpets, and some carpet manufacturers' warranties won't insure the carpet if you use a desiccant powder. Also, neither you nor your dog should inhale the powder, which can physically (rather than chemically) damage the lungs. Use a dust respirator when applying.

There are a number of powders and sprays that utilize pungent herbs or essential oils intended to drive fleas away. Eucalyptus is a common ingredient, as is peppermint. But unless these products are used in an overwhelming concentration, or in combination with other remedies, they are unlikely to be effective.

If your dog habitually sleeps in one or two areas, or has a bed, cover those spots with a towel or a small, washable blanket. Immersion in water kills both eggs and developing flea larvae, so wash the bedding every other day or so. Some people keep two or three sets of towels for bedding so the dog's favorite spot is always covered—keeping the trap set constantly, as it were, for flea eggs.

Wash uncarpeted floors at least once a week. Wood floors are especially important to wash well, since the larvae tend to burrow into cracks in the wood. Similarly, steam cleaners (used without chemicals) can kill flea eggs and larvae present in short carpets. You probably couldn't (or wouldn't want to) get thick rugs wet enough to kill the eggs, however.

# Taking the War Outside

Outdoors, it's easier to use water to your advantage. Most dogs pick out a couple of spots in shady or protected areas where they spend most of their time in your yard. Fleas, too, like these shady spots; in fact, neither the adult fleas nor the larvae can survive very long in direct sunlight. It's unnecessary, then, to worry about the lion's share of the landscaping or lawn areas around your house. At least once a week, wash down the areas your dog uses for sleeping and resting.

Other safe tools you can use in the outdoor flea war are beneficial nematodes, tiny creatures that seek out and kill fleas. Several companies raise and sell the nematodes, which are strictly insectivorous and cannot harm humans, pets, plants, or the beneficial earthworms in your garden.

Application of the nematodes is simple. About one million nematodes come packaged on a small sponge pad, about 2-3 inches square. The sponge is soaked in about a gallon of water, and then the water is sprayed over the area to be treated. The nematodes should be distributed at night or on a cloudy day, since they die if exposed to direct sunlight. They also work best in a moist environment, so watering the yard well for several weeks after application helps them do their job most efficiently.

Suggest use is about one million nematodes per every 2500 square feet of garden or yard. Does this sound like a lot? Don't worry! Costs range between $1-15 per million, depending on the source and quantity purchased. ❣

# 26

# Canine Car Safety

*Babies and small children must be protected
with car seats and seat belts.
Why not dogs, too?*

There are seat belt laws in most states now, and young children are legally required to be restrained in safety seats in cars in all states. But nowhere is there a law requiring dogs to be safely contained in vehicles. Those that do only address restraint for dogs in the back of open pick-up trucks.

Nor are there statistics available for the number of dogs killed or injured in automobile accidents each year. Dr. Joseph Evans, DVM, of Nederland, Colorado reports that, in a single year, he has seen as many as 91 dogs injured in auto acccidents, of which 13 died. Of the 40,000-plus persons killed each year in the U.S. in car accidents, 45 percent might been saved by seat belts; seat belts also may have reduced serious injuries by 50 percent. Logically, they'd do the same for pets.

The forces generated by even a low-speed collision are tremendous and can be expressed in various ways. If a car is doing 40 mph, unrestrained occupants will continue forward motion at that speed until they hit something. The impact of a 25 mph accident is often compared to falling from a three-story window; in a 30 mph crash, g-forces convert a 20-pound baby into a 600-pound mass; at the same speed, a 60-pound dog will impact an object within a foot with a force of 1,000 pounds per square inch. Any car restraint must be able to withstand these forces to protect the occupant.

The federal standard for a two-inch seat belt is 6,000 pounds of tensile strength.There are no standards for canine restraints, although—to be effective—they must conform to the laws of physics.

Unfortunately, according to tensile testing we conducted, many of the restraints we obtained seemed incapable of resisting the forces that likely would be encountered in a low- to moderate-speed collision. However, a few did seem to measure up.

Not all of the restraints examined are intended to serve as seatbelts. Several suppliers, in their disclaimers, note that the primary use of their device is to keep a pet under control while riding in the car. That itself is a safety factor, as witness the accident involving writer Stephen King, who was injured while walking along a road when a pickup truck driver, trying to corral his unrestrained Rottweiler, lost control of his vehicle. (From the dog's point of view, even when safely restrained in the back of a truck, the potential for severe injury is great. Consider the risk of damage to eyes from flying debris, the discomfort from exposure to the elements, the encouragement of aggressive dog behavior, and the real possibility of jumping or falling from the truck.)

Another purpose served by restraints is to prevent your dog from becoming a flying missile in the event of an accident—something that could be dangerous for both the animal and passengers.

Restraints are also helpful, as with humans, in protecting pets from the explosive force of an airbag—although it's safest to strap your dog in on the back seat. Finally, restraints can aid rescue personnel, who report being held off or attacked by unrestrained and panicked dogs while attempting to perform their duties at the scene of an accident.

# Canine Car Restraints

## What we looked for:

We examined all the belts carefully, looked at any enclosed instructions, and tried them out for fit—first on a large stuffed dog (in a sitting position), then on some real, live animals. We looked at the quality of the fabric, the stitching, and the hardware, but, most importantly, looked for any flaws in the design, any weak links that might cause a given device to fail under pressure. As the National Highway Transportation Safety Administration has noted, any car safety restraint is only as strong as its weakest link.

Nylon webbing itself is extremely strong, including the individual fibers, according to those in the industry. So is stitching, properly done with good thread. Even the one-inch webbing used in some of the restraints should withstand several thousand pounds of force, possibly more. In none of our testing did any of the nylon sections, regardless of size or thickness, fail when we brought them to the maximum load; nor did they show signs of distress afterwards. We'd venture that any of the sewn or tacked nylon components we looked at is capable of restraining an animal in a crash.

With several of the harnesses, it seemed, to our eye, that connection points—i.e., buckles or shackles—would bear much of the load instead of the nylon webbing. These we took (along with the others, for general evaluation) to the University of Rhode Island textile lab, which has a tensile-strength test machine, a QTest I Sintech. This machine can exert a top load of 1,000 pounds, at a top speed of 20 inches per second. This is far from a shock-load or a high-end pull strength to test ultimate breaking power. That was not our intention.

Our premise was to seek out any inherent weaknesses in the design or construction of the restraints, at forces far less than would be at play in an actual collision. In some cases, we obtained just one sample of a given brand, creating a theoretical possibility that we had in hand a defective anomaly. However, we doubt that's the case. While there were a few surprises, most of the restraints that failed did so in the location we expected them to fail. Here are our evaluations.

# Basic Types

There are two basic types of restraints: the canine safety harness, and the canine car seat. Note that all these systems utilize car seat belts. In many of today's cars, the front seat belts (and some rear belts) only tighten on impact; during normal travel they expand to allow for passenger comfort. In order to securely fasten any canine restraint system, you may have to use a rear, solid belt or come up with an alternate strap around the front seat to provide a stable base for the attachment. Unless you are mechanically proficient, we would recommend having a solid seat belt installed by a professional.

## Harnesses

■ **Ruff Rider "Roadie":** This was the the beefiest of the harness restraints we looked at, and the only one that was subjected to tensile-strength testing by an independent laboratory According to the lab report, the Ruff Rider in several pulls on a Tinius Olsen machine, failed at 6,675 and 7025 pounds, which meets and exceeds human belt standards—very impressive, especially when you consider the average dog is much lighter than a human.

The Ruff Rider comes with detailed explanations—10 drawings along the side of the box—that show how to put the harness on a

188 ■ THE GOOD DOG LIBRARY

dog. Nevertheless, we felt like we had a fistful of spaghetti when we first picked it up. That's because there's a bit more to this harness than some of the others. It's daunting but not that complicated if you follow the directions carefully. And if this becomes your harness of choice, putting it on will quickly become second nature.

The Roadie has a number of strong points. The 1-3/4-inch nylon webbing that makes up the major stress routes puts it up into the human category of seatbelts. With seatbelts, wider is better—more comfortable to wear and more comfortable when you strain against it under force. We also like the way the belt criss-crosses on the chest and is heavily pleated and tacked about the shoulders where it connects with a car's seat belt system.

The harness itself is a one-piece device; 1-inch nylon webbing straps, along with Delrin side-release buckles, permit adjustments at the belly and chest. Proper fit is important, as the instructions note; according to the National Highway Traffic Safety Administration, improper fit (including twisted straps) can negate the protection provided by a restraint.

The Ruff Rider is our top choice; it's a well-thought-out, ruggedly-made restraint that should do the job it's designed for.

■ **Pet Safe-T-Belt**: The most expensive of the harnesses we tested, the Pet Safe-T-Belt is also the sturdiest, consisting of a body harness, frame attachment, and front seat strap, it comes in four sizes ranging from toy dog size (3-7 lbs.), to large breeds (51-100 lbs.). It is completely adjustable, and made of strong, soft nylon, with stitching and fasteners on the outside, away from contact with the pet, to minimize rubbing. It is a bit complicated to assemble and install.

While exceptionally secure, the dual-sided-restraint design caused our test dog some anxiety by unduly restricting her movement. This is a good choice for owners who want a high-end sturdy product and are willing to help their dogs adjust to its high level of restraint.

■ **Batzibelt**: One of the simplest dog restraints, designed to work with a dog's own harness, the Batzibelt consists of a length of 1-inch nylon webbing with a swivel shackle at each end. One end snaps to the dog's harness (NEVER the collar), the other to the Batzi's second component, a triangular shackle which clips onto the car's existing seat belt, and which can be left there. Simplicity and ease of use are the main selling points.

We were concerned about the length of the Batzi's lead, however, which, combined with any forward motion of the car belt, might cause a dog to strike the dashboard or the back of a front seat (depending on where the dog is sitting). We'd recommend that any reader take measurements in his or her own car and gauge how much distance there is between their dog's head and a solid structure before considering any restraint that includes a lead.

Our editors also were concerned about the integrity of the hardware, specifically the cast-steel swivel shackles. In our first test, the D-ring portion of the shackle snapped at 700 pounds after about 5 seconds of pulling; on a second Batzi, the head of the shackle shattered at 392 pounds

■ **Quick Stay**: This is similar in makeup and design to the Batzibelt, with an added feature: a "Snap-Back" length of elastic cord (like a bungee) that is intended to act as a shock absorber. The car restraint evolved from the manufacturer's Snap-Back training leashes. A disclaimer on the package states that the consumer understands that the Quick Stay's primary function is to keep a pet from wandering about a vehicle and that the maker offers no warranty of protection in the event of an accident.

The Quick Stay is made of 1-inch nylon webbing (a 20-inch length in the large size) and is adjustable via a plastic slide buckle; at one end is a D-ring and snap shackle—the part of the strap with the D-ring slips around a fastened seat belt and is clipped in place with the shackle. At the other end, the Snap-Back cord is doubled around a second D-Ring and fastened to the shackle that attaches to the dog.

We tested the Quick Stay on the QTest machine, and the bungee stretched to the limits of the machine without breaking, although the cover did disintegrate. But the great capacity of the shock cord to stretch kept the actual load to just 132 pounds; the Snap-Back, then, does its job of absorbing energy.

The downside is that the stretching, combined with the length of the nylon lead, means a dog would be propelled very far forward in the event of a serious crash and would almost certainly impact with some part of the car.

The Quick-Stay, according to the manufacturer, can also be used as a street leash (fine) or to secure a dog in a truck bed (not so fine).

■ **Easy Rider** (formerly Safari): This is now distributed by Coastal Pet Products, marketers of the Halti head harness.The single, and rather large, buckle  serves to secure the harness at the back of the dog's neck.

Leg and girth straps are 1-inch nylon webbing, while the loop that goes over the car seat belt and is secured via two D-rings to the harness measures 1-7/8 inches; there's a vertical padded strap on the front (which we like) that is 2 inches wide. Instructions are adequate, and the harness goes on fairly easily, over the head and the two front legs. As with any unfamiliar gear, Coastal suggests that you put the car harness on your dog several times so he can get used it, then go for a short drive. If you must leave your dog in the car for a bit and it's the excitable type, the instructions suggest that you undo the safety belt until you return.

## Car seats

The selection among canine car seats is limited at best. We evaluated three, and found only one acceptable. For small dogs the car seat can provide an effective restraint system, but it is not an option for larger dogs.

■ **The Dog-Gone Device**: If you have a small dog (20 pounds or less), and like to carry your dog as much as drive him or her around, this carrier is for you.

The Dog-Gone is primarily a backpack-style animal carrier that doubles as a car seat. Its adjustable mesh fabric pouch is attached to a lightweight frame. Four restraint loops hold the dog's collar as the dog sits in an upright position, and an extending leg allows the device to stand on its own as long as the dog is sitting still.

No installation is required; the carrier is simply placed on the seat of the car and strapped in by the seat belt around it. A seat belt that stays tight is mandatory to prevent the carrier from tipping over when you brake.

The Dog-Gone Device might be a kick for owners who want to take their little dogs with them for errands or other short trips, but don't want to travel at a little dog's pace.

But as a car seat only, it leaves room for improvement. The dog is held upright and can't lie down. We would only recommend it as a car seat for short trips. Any dog would find it too confining for longer drives.

## Modified leashes

We found several products that were essentially modified leashes, intended to be used with a dog's usual harness or collar. Please note that we do not recommend attaching a vehicle restraint strap to your dog's collar as the primary means of restraint.

Although this would work to keep him contained during normal travel, in an accident the force of impact could damage the dog's trachea, injure the spine, perhaps even break his neck. For just a few dollars more you can purchase the Pet Safety Sitter, for example, and know that your dog is safely and securely restrained.

## Not recommended

■ **Top Paws' Safe N-Go**: This harness is obviously a low-end product. The nylon is narrow, stiff, and the plastic snaps and metal hard-

*The Dog-Gone car seat/backpack is a handy accessory for owners of small dogs. But since the dog must travel upright in the carrier, its use should be limited to short sessions for the dog's comfort. Also, when used as a car seat, the belts used to secure the seat should be the kind that lock into adjustment. If the belt adjustment slides, the seat could tip.*

ware are cheap. The packaging doesn't indicate which size harness is contained inside, and the instructions for use are cryptic, ungrammatical and hard to follow.

■ **Foster & Smith's ComfortRide Pet Seat**: Although it is well-made and able to accommodate larger dogs, the ComfortRide Pet Seat relies on restraint via the dog's collar, which could result in serious damage to the dog's neck in an accident.

■ **Four Paws**: In our pull test, both buckles parted simultaneously at 440 pounds after a little more than three seconds; one broke at the base of the prongs, the other at the base of the female receptacle.

■ **Premier Sure-Fit Harness**: It has several good points: It's easy to put on—intuitive almost—although there is a reference picture on the packaging; it's adjustable in a variety of ways, and the stress points are at the strong points (the plastic buckles are for positioning and fixing in place, rather than taking the brunt of a sudden stop). The harness combines with a "car control snap" that features a loop, through which to pass the car seat belt, with a quality bronze swivel shackle, which can double as a short leash. However, the lead creates the same extension problems as the Batzi and Quick Stay.

On the minus side, the nylon webbing, at just 3/4-inch wide, is too narrow, in our opinion, for a restraint strap. Company disclaimers make it clear that this product has not been "crash-tested" and is intended mainly as a device for restraining your pet underway. As such, it's not in the same league as some of the hardier harnesses that aspire to provide collision protection.

■ **Hunter**: The harness comes together at the back of the shoulders, in a manner similar to the Ruff Rider, except this is where the connecting hardware also joins. The system makes clever use of two interlocking polycarbonate-like triangles, one with a protruding steel tongue, which connects to a buckle receptacle. The design means that this critical junction point will take the initial (and full) momentum caused by an abrupt stop or collision; thus, if any of the components fail, the whole system goes. Second negative: the part of the tongue that protrudes (and enters the lock) is only 7/8-inch long (compared to 1-1/2 inches on a human seat belt), and difficult to lock into place, which someone in a hurry could fail to do properly. In our first pull on the QTest machine, the tongue popped from its catch with an audible pop at 600 pounds, after about 3 seconds; on a second pull, the buckle popped again, this time at only 377 pounds. Unfortunately, we do not trust the essential connection/stress point and cannot recommend this restraint.

# Conclusions/Recommendations

Although we probably did not find all the restraints on the market, of those we did the Ruff Rider Roadie was clearly the superior product, in the opinion of the editors, well-made and without any design or construction defects that we could detect. While not in the same category, the relatively inexpensive Easy Rider harness should do an adequate job of securing your pet while offering restraint in the event of an accident. But for maximum protection, we recommend spending the extra money for the Ruff Rider. ❧

# 27

# Preventing "Lost Dog"

*One of the kindest things you can do for your dog is
provide it with proper identification.
We suggest multiple IDs to prevent
every owner's worst nightmare.*

L osing a canine companion is a responsible dog owner's worst nightmare. We go to great lengths to ensure our dogs' safety. We leash them, fence them, keep them indoors, or close to our sides. Yet accidents happen. A door doesn't close tightly. The meter reader leaves the gate open. A section of fence falls down in a windstorm, flood, or earthquake. We're in a car accident and our dog panics, jumps through the broken windshield and runs off. While safe, appropriate confinement is a critical first-line defense against pet loss, proper identification is your lost dog's "ticket" home when the first line fails. It's one of the most caring things you can do for your dog, and one of the first things you should do when you acquire your new pet.

## But Which Kind of Identification?

There are actually just three primary types for dogs—ID tags, tattooing, and microchips; each has its advantages and disadvantages.

### ID tags
Most citizens who find a dog will promptly contact the owner and return the dog home if they can. An ID tag gives the finder immediate information and facilitates a speedy reunion, saving a trip to the nearest animal shelter and forestalling hours or days of anxious search-

ing by the owner. A license can do the same after one quick call to animal control to get owner information. Many animal control agencies also have a policy of trying to return a dog home rather than impounding him, if he is wearing a current license or ID. Since most agencies charge impound and board fees to reclaim impounded animals (fees can sometimes exceed $100), the ID tag can also save an owner anxiety, by preempting a costly trip to the shelter.

There is a wide variety of ID tags to choose from, and it probably doesn't matter which you use, as long as you use one of them. Temporary paper-and-plastic tags can be filled out with a permanent marker and then sealed, allowing for instant security. You can send away for fancy engraved tags that will never fade or suffer water damage. There are even "talking" ID tags that play a recorded message to your dog's rescuer.

Because tags provide potential for the quickest trip home for your dog, most shelter officials vehemently urge that dogs wear ID tags and licenses at all times, as the mainstay of an identification program, even when the dog is safe at home.

Make your choice based on your and your dog's needs—immediacy, durability and fashion statement—and then consider the added protection of the two backup methods of ID, because the ID tag is not the perfect solution. Tags and collars can fall off, or can be removed by unfriendly people.

Also, some owners don't like to use them due to the annoyance of the jingling of tags as the dog moves around, or scratches at an errant flea. While the annoyance seems minor in comparison to the trauma of losing a dog, an easy solution to this complaint is to tape or rivet the tags flat against the collar, or to buy a flat leather collar to which a flat ID tag is riveted.

## Tattoos

Tattooing takes the collar ID concept one step further, by giving the dog a form of un-removable (and silent!) identification. It involves the injection of ink under the dog's skin with an electronic pen. When the tattoo technician "writes" with the pen, a tiny needle injects the ink to a depth of 1/32 of an inch under the skin, in a series of numbers or letters. According to Julie Muscove, founder and executive director of Tatoo-A-Pet, the procedure is quick and painless.

"We sell the system to veterinarians, groomers, breeders, and other authorized agents, at a cost of about $250," she says."Although it doesn't require the use of anesthesia, most vets will anesthetize the dog because they find it easier to work on a stationary target than a moving one. So the cost of tattooing may range from $20 from an authorized agent (who doesn't anesthetize) to more than $100 from some veterinarians."

Tattoos are usually placed on the bare skin inside a dog's flank, or sometimes, as in the case of racing greyhounds, in the dog's ear. Tattoos cannot be lost or removed, and they are pretty durable, although someone can alter a tattoo if they are determined. (Horror stories of greyhounds having their tattooed ear cut off and then being abandoned have sickened the dog world gossip circuit; for this reason alone, Tatoo-A-Pet does not recommend tattooing the ears.) Tattoos can be a great way to prove ownership in a custody or identity dispute, and laboratories are generally leery of doing research on tattooed dogs without first tracing ownership.

The tattoo dilemma has to do with what you choose to write. In today's transient society, a phone number is no good; a person might move several times in their dog's life, or area codes can change. Some owners tattoo their pets with their Social Security number (SSN) or driver's license number, but these, too, are problematic. For security reasons, neither Social Security nor state drivers' licensing officials will release a person's address or phone number. Local police departments and city animal shelters which are affiliated with the local police departments can access driver's license information and contact the owners, but they cannot trace Social Security numbers.

There are at least two national dog tattoo registries that can facilitate tattoo tracing, but finding an owner can still be a frustrating proposition, since not all owners registers their dogs' tattoos with one of or both of these two groups. The companies are aware of the system's shortcomings, and they do what they can to overcome them.

■ **Tatoo-A-Pet**, which has been in operation for 26 years, will help trace any tattoo, not just those registered with them. To make the registration attractive, they charge just $10 to register a tattoo for each pet's lifetime, or a one-time $25 fee for a multiple-pet household. The company claims a 99 percent tattoo recovery success rate.

■ **National Dog Registry** is another leading tattoo registry that helps people find qualified tattoo technicians in their area, and will register any letter or number combination, but suggests that their clients lead the chosen combination with "NDR." Of course, this approach depends on recognition of the NDR initials and name.

■ **Petfinders** is another dog-registration company that has made a specialty out of registering dog descriptions. While the presence of a tattoo certainly aids the description that the company will enter in their database of dog descriptions, they will also register dogs without tattoos.

*Identification tags come in numerous forms—metal, plastic, instant, mail-order, cute, and utilitarian. It doesn't matter which you use, as long as you have one on your dogs at all times.*

If you have a pure-bred dog, the American Kennel Club recommends tattooing it with its AKC registration number. The Club has established a unit, the Companion Animal Recovery, that will assist a registered dog become reunited with its rightful owner. Critics of the Club allege that the Club's records on owners' names, addresses, and phone numbers are notoriously out of date and incomplete, and can be next to useless.

A final frustration is that most shelters don't routinely roll incoming dogs onto their backs to look for tattoos. Many dogs don't take kindly to being rolled on their backs by a stranger, especially in the high-stress environment of an animal shelter, and shelters are understandably reluctant to risk bites to staff from dogs who protest the procedure. However, most shelters, but by no means all, will make an effort to look for tattoos immediately prior to euthanasia, if a dog will tolerate the search.

## Microchipping

The third dog identification option is microchipping, also known as "radio frequency identification." The high-tech member of the dog ID team has been available commercially for companion animal identification since 1988.

The microchip is a tiny computer chip etched with an identification code. The chip is attached to an antenna and encased in surgical-grade glass to form a transponder, or tag. The transponder is about the size of a grain of rice, and when injected under the skin between a dog's shoulder blades, is unnoticeable on all but the smallest and most short-haired dogs. The injection process takes only a few seconds, requires no anesthesia, and is no more painful for a pet than a vaccination.

A special receiver is used to "read" the chip's transponder by use of a tiny radio frequency signal. Shelter staff scanning a lost pet can use the code to locate the owner of the animal, or to retrieve any other information stored in the system's database. The life expectancy of the chip is 20 to 25 years, and the cost of chipping is affordable to most pet owners—from $15 at some animal shelters, to $50 or more at veterinary hospitals, with an additional cost for lifetime registration in some system databases.

A permanent, unalterable method of pet identification sounds almost too good to be true, and of course, it is. The "Big Brother" aspect of microchipping makes some people uncomfortable. Some holistic veterinarians and owners cringe at the idea of permanently injecting a foreign object, albeit a tiny one, under the dog's skin. (However, there is no documented evidence to show that chips present any kind of health risk to dogs.)

More significant are the kind of drawbacks that challenge the efficacy of the tattoo system. Not all shelters scan for chips, so some chip companies offer a visible ID tag to alert finders that the pet is chipped. Of course, the tag can be lost or removed. It is also possible to miss a chip while scanning, although over the last decade the quality of scanners has improved. Fractious animals can be difficult to scan. Microchip manufacturers are working to invent newer, better technology.

# Infighting Slows Progress

But perhaps the most serious downside on the microchip scene is the squabbling between the three major players in microchip marketing. Destron manufactures the "Home Again" chip, which is marketed to veterinarians through Scheuring-Plough. Destron's database is kept by the AKC's Companion Animal Recovery division. Avid markets their own microchip and maintains their own database. InfoPet initially marketed the Destron chip, but now sells the Trovan chip, manufactured in Europe, and also maintains their own database.

Lawsuits and accusations between the companies over proprietary information abound, which gives rise to concerns about the stability and longevity of the various companies and their registration systems. The infighting has also slowed the progress toward universally compatible systems, much to the detriment of lost pet recovery. If shelter staff doesn't have access to all three scanners, they may find themselves unable to access the necessary information, even if they know a chip is present in a dog. Although at least one company claims to have a "universal" scanner that reads all three companies' chips and the others report that theirs will at least identify the presence of another chip, the reliability of the scanners reportedly declines when they are used to scan for chips other than their own.

If your local shelters have a well-developed chipping program (as is the case in many parts of California), then this method may be a viable element of your dog identification package. In 1989, the Marin Humane Society, in Novato, California, became the first shelter in the country to microchip all of their adoption dogs and cats; the shelter now also offers chipping services to the general public at an extremely low cost. Shelter staff say they recover close to 200 microchipped dogs each year, many of whom are not wearing any other form of identification, despite the fact that every adoption animal leaves the shelter wearing a physical ID tag.

# Lost Dog Checklist

## First
■ *Call local police, animal-control officer, and animal shelter(s).*
■ *Call all tag, tattoo, or microchip registries with which you have registered your dog.*
■ *Alert your neighbors.*
■ *Mobilize friends to begin an immediate search.*
■ *Make sure your answering machine is on.*
■ *Leave the fence gate open so he can return on his own.*
■ *Place items with your scent in the dog's crate, and leave the crate where the dog was last seen.*

## Next
■ *Call the state police or highway patrol, along with sheriffs, animal-control officers, police departments, and animal shelters in surrounding towns.*
■ *Notify all area emergency animal hospitals that you guarantee payment for treatment if your dog is found and brought in.*
■ *Keep a list of all people and organizations you contact, with phone numbers.*

■ *Create and distribute a flyer with all pertinent information, including a clear photograph of your dog and a reward offer.*
■ *Visit nearby animal shelters to look for your dog.*

### Follow-up

■ *Produce a professional-looking poster. Post it and send a copy to everyone you called.*
■ *Place ads offering a reward in local papers; take advantage of local TV and radio lost-pet announcements if available.*
■ *Keep in touch with everyone you contacted in the beginning.*
■ *After you've found your dog, call all your contacts to let them know your canine friend is safe and sound. They'll appreciate it.*

# The ID Answer?

The best approach to identification is to cover all the bases. Certainly, all pets should wear ID tags at all times, not just when they are out for a walk. But in the event that tags are lost or removed, a back-up tattoo and/or a microchip, especially if they are registered with one or more registries, can literally mean the difference between life and death for your missing pet.

"We recommend using all three methods," says Kat Brown, Director of Operations for the Santa Cruz SPCA. "A regular ID tag is most helpful for the finder. A chip is great back-up when you have shelters and vets in your area that scan. A tattoo is triple insurance." In other words, why not give your dog two or three "tickets" home? ❧

# Section III

Grooming

# 28

# Grooming the Pooch You Love

*Primary reasons for grooming dogs are health and cleanliness. Here's how to make it an enjoyable experience for both of you.*

When Emma, a German Shepherd mix with magnificent, mule deer ears, jumps out of the car after being driven home from a particularly hard run on the trails or mucky outing at the beach, she immediately trots into the bathroom and waits for her bath. During her soaping and rinsing, her owner sings and tells her stories. Cheeky squirrels are given a run for their money by fleet, wily dogs. Cats are put firmly in their place by commanding, resourceful dogs, and humans are rescued from various perils by brave and sagacious dogs—all of whom bear a striking resemblance to Emma, of course.

After an initial toweling and shake, Emma is wrapped in a warm cotton flannel blanket and snuggles under the bedclothes to take a long nap. When she awakens, refreshed and sweet- smelling, she is brushed, extravagantly praised and given a special treat.

For Emma, life—and being groomed—is a very good thing, indeed. Grooming Emma is also a pleasure for Emma's owner: An intimate interlude in a hectic day spent caring for and paying attention to someone dear to her heart. They've worked out their ritual to their own satisfaction and they both love it.

From toenails to teeth to tail, grooming is an intimate, personal issue. We groom our dogs for their health and cleanliness and the satisfaction of seeing them look their best.

However, "best" is a relative term and whatever it means to you, it can be difficult to achieve when something is amiss in the canine/human relationship. Precisely because grooming is such an intimate act, the process can invoke physical pain (an aching back, for instance), as well as feelings of impatience, frustration, and guilt in both groomer and groomee!

# Forget Quick Fixes

Grooming your dog when you're disgruntled, or procrastinating and avoiding the issue, are like abusing credit cards: you may get what you want now, but you can't avoid having to pay the bill—with interest—later. Your dog pays with a reduction in her health and an increase in her stress and discomfort. You pay with time and money spent at the groomer's or veterinarian's office. Your relationship with your dog also suffers from a breach of trust.

Your dog also has her own perceptions and feelings about being groomed. One dog may balk and back away from the bathroom door. Another may gouge the floor during her great escape from a nail trim. A third may tremble in tune with an aspen leaf at the sight of a flea comb.

Attempts to groom under these circumstances can not only exacerbate a problem, but set up a mutually damaging cycle: the more she resists, the more you'll dislike grooming her. The more you shirk this duty, the more likely she'll develop some of the very conditions grooming helps to prevent.

The primary reasons for grooming your dog are health and cleanliness. One benefit is that skin conditions, lumps, and injuries can be noticed and treated by you, or by a veterinarian if necessary.

Neglecting to groom your dog can cause skin problems and pain from dirty and matted fur, gait problems and joint stress from overlong toenails, hearing loss from clogged or damaged ears, local and systemic infections from gingivitis, and any number of health problems from undetected and untreated flea and tick infestations.

# Positive Vibrations

If you're not grooming your dog on a regular basis, you and your dog can break the cycle and get back in harmony by working to change each other's perceptions about grooming. As the groomer, you are responsible for your dog's experience. In order to bring about a more perfect union of trust, harmony, and balance, you need to take the first step.

Begin by remembering when you and your dog shared a wonderful moment of complete trust, companionship, and harmony. Then try to maintain that feeling while you imagine grooming your dog. It may seem impossible to have those feelings during a grooming session, but read on! It's not just possible—it can even be fun!

# Touching with Love

Grooming is based on touch more than anything else we do with and to our dogs. It's impossible to accomplish any of it without touching your dog, whether it's toenail trimming or tooth-brushing, flea combing, or untangling matted fur, a quick lick and a promise or a laborious show "do." No matter how you define it, feel about it, or do it, grooming is a non-verbal form of communication that is transmitted through touch.

Helen Keller expressed this wonderfully: "I have just touched my dog. He was rolling on the grass with pleasure in every muscle and limb. I wanted to catch a picture of him in my fingers, and I touched him as lightly as I would a cobweb...he pressed close to me, as if he were fain to crowd himself into my hand...if he could speak, I believe he would say with me that paradise is attained by touch, for in touch is all love and intelligence."

To groom your dog with the touch of love and intelligence, to "catch a picture" of her in your fingers through touch— that is communication. What you say and do with her and how you "listen" to what she's saying and doing creates a feedback loop that results in an ever-more-meaningful and expansive conversation that replaces the old cycle of irritation, pain, and mistrust. Being willing to change our attitudes and approaches to grooming, and to help our dogs become cooperative participants, is a great start toward creating a rewarding ritual rather than a habitual pattern of balk/pull, whine/admonish, cower/encourage, yay/whew!

This is where techniques such as TTouch can be most helpful. If the theorists about the body/mind connection are right (and recent discoveries in neurology and cellular biology indicate they are), the body remembers everything that happens to it. TTouch works directly on the nervous system to help you to discover the response patterns stored in your dog's (and your) body and bring them to the brain's attention. When the brain can perceive a more efficient way to function, it makes every effort to implement it. Improvements in health and behavior can be rapid and permanent. The dog's ability to think and focus is increased.

Bringing awareness to how your dog (and you) hides or express-es responses is an opportunity for you to interrupt habitual, nega-tive patterns and point the way to new, more positive ones. This helps change how the body feels about itself and, along with relief from fear, tension, and stress, creates a better self-image and boosts self-esteem. The benefits are reciprocal and balance is achieved.

Creating these new feelings, added to your new perceptions, will profoundly change the way you communicate with your dog. The term "handling" will take on a whole new meaning. Your relation-ship will thrive and harmony will be restored.

# Grooming Goals

■ *I will groom my dog for her health and cleanliness.*
■ *I will cause her no harm in the process.*
■ *I will make it as mutually pleasurable as possible.*

*Explore these statements with mindful awareness and imagination. With this credo and TTouch in hand, your choice of methods, tools, and techniques will become self-evident as an expression of your philosophy, creativi-ty, and attitude. When difficulties arise your new percep-tion will lead you to ask questions. Why is this happen-ing? How can I help? You will find new and ingenious solutions.*

# A New Beginning

To start anew, pretend you've never groomed your dog before. With a note pad and pen, sit down and without side comments or judg-ments, look at your dog with fresh eyes. What's her body type? Is she delicate, sturdy, long, lean, short, round, tiny, or huge?

Think about her emotional and physical sensitivity. Is she a shrink-ing Violet, nervous Nellie, swooning Camille, or the Rock of Gibral-tar? Note what kind of coat she has. Is it thick, thin, long, short, fine, coarse, swirly, wavy, or straight?

Remind yourself about how she approaches things. Does she like to have advance notice, be talked through difficulties, mull them over, negotiate, or be bribed? Highlight any special issues. Is she in-experienced, energetic, old, infirm, allergic, disabled, or phobic?

Now imagine her going through the grooming process. Do you anticipate any glitches? Looking over your list of her emotional and physical considerations, can you think of any things you could do to make the process go more smoothly, more pleasurably for her— and for you? With notes in hand and fresh insights in mind, make a grooming plan for your dog.

Evaluate her grooming environment. Think about temperatures, surfaces, sounds, smells, and feelings. Think about her safety and comfort for each stage. Think about where you're starting and where you want to end up. Put yourself in her place and try the tools and techniques on yourself! Imagine yourself going through a similar process at a spa, as a young child and as an invalid; how would you like to be handled?

Separate each grooming task and then break it down even further. One nail clipped successfully (from her viewpoint) on Monday will give you a big advantage when you go to clip the next one on Tuesday. Small steps now will lead to major accomplishments tomorrow.

Timing is everything. Choose your time wisely and give yourself plenty of it. Take your dog's daily routines and your schedule into account. Better a job left undone than one done in a hurry or just before she goes out for her midday dirt roll! Ask yourself whether you

*Use a wide-toothed comb or pick on mats or thick fur and start from the ends and work toward the skin. A comb with rotating teeth works well in sensitive areas such as behind the ears or on dogs like Playa who have very fine or thick tangled hair. Use round-tipped scissors for mats that can't be combed out easily.*

have time to complete the task and whether it is reasonable to do so. Remember, not everything has to be done at once.

Be prepared. Make sure you have everything you need for the job at hand. A check list for each job can be a handy reminder in the beginning. Turn off the phone or at least bring it with you. This is a special time for you and your dog. It's rude, as well as potentially very messy, to let yourself be distracted by something. Picture a soaped up dog running through the house and you won't have any trouble staying focused!

Pay attention. Breathe, start slowly, and be fully present. Monitor your dog; if she starts to have a problem, stop as quickly as possible and end with something enjoyable. Use products she likes and what's easy for her; change what she doesn't like or what is difficult for her. "Bracket" things she's not sure about with very good things before and after. If you make the endings really wonderful (think of Emma), your dog will know what's coming next and look forward to it.

Separate training or practice from the real thing. Use the word "bath" only when you really mean it. She may act like a clown to distract you or avoid being touched in a sensitive area, but don't tease, threaten, or laugh at her. You're both finding your way to a better place, so be patient and explain to her what you're doing and why. It's only polite to do so and she may surprise you with her understanding response. Ginger, an Australian Shepherd I know, once surprised her owner this way. When told it was really difficult to reach the mat on the inside of her thigh, Ginger lifted her leg and patiently held it up until the job was done.

Read books, watch videos, pick the brains of professional groomers and competent friends, and peruse catalogues for new tools and general information about dogs and grooming. There's a better grooming mouse trap every day!

# Grooming Tips, Tricks, and Touches

Long, slow strokes over the whole body can calm and prepare a dog for grooming. If she is very nervous, use the back of the hand, a gently curled fist, or a fleece polishing glove to soften the contact.

■ A sewing seam and thread cutter works well to separate and cut mats.

■ Use brushes with rounded tips to protect sensitive skin. Think about recreating a beauty parlor when brushing! Try humming or singing to establish a relaxing rhythm.

■ Specialized grooming tools are helpful, but not always necessary. If you can't find a comb, you can use a fork for working out mats; baking soda on a damp sponge for reducing odors, and Vaseline or vegetable oil for gooey things like tar.

■ Use round tipped scissors to cut mats or tangles without cutting the skin. Use a comb between the skin and the mat to protect the skin from pointy scissors. Cornstarch, vegetable oil, or conditioner can be used on mats to soften and make them easier to comb out.

## Bathing

■ Place a towel on the living room floor and do everything you would do in the tub—without the water and shampoo. Go slowly and reward your dog often.

■ To get her into the bathroom, lure your dog with treats, reward her, and let her go out again. To get her in the tub, put the treats on the rim, then on the bottom. Do several times in one day, then add turning on the sink water. Then put the treats at one end of the tub and turn the water on slowly at the other. Let her go if she wants and gradually increase time and water amount.

■ For small, elderly, or arthritic dogs, use a stool or ramp to help them get in and out of a tub. Cover it and the tub bottom with non-skid material. Towels work well when wet. Dry her feet well if your floors are slippery.

■ Putting a soft visor on your dog's head will help keep soap and water out of his eyes and ears.

■ If possible, put a small stool in the tub with your dog and sit on that; your back will thank you! Small dogs can be washed in the kitchen sink or on a table with two rubber tubs one for washing, one for the final rinsing.

■ Keep your dog in the tub with peanut butter, cream cheese, or butter smeared on the end wall for her to lick. For brushing, smear the food on the refrigerator or sprinkle treats on the floor.

■ For itchy or broken skin use an oatmeal-based shampoo or make your own oatmeal rinse. Whiz one cup of dry oatmeal in a blender and then soak it in two quarts of water for ten minutes. Strain and add half a cup of aloe vera. For fleas, add a teaspoon of citrus oil.

■ Miracle Groom cleans, deodorizes, repels fleas, and soothes the skin. Its natural ingredients don't need water. Just spray it on your dog, your hands, or a towel, rub in and wipe off. It's a great addition for your car kit and those muddy and she-rolled-in-something-yucky days.

■ Always use dog shampoo; dogs' skin is more alkaline than ours. Using simple and natural ingredients will minimize allergic reactions or exacerbation of an existing skin condition.

■ Rinse, rinse, rinse, and dry with a chamois or sports towel.

■ For a dry shampoo, use cornstarch, oatmeal whizzed in a blender, talcum powder, or fullers earth. Rub in well and brush against the fur to remove oil and dirt. Put cotton balls in the ear to keep out water;  add a little oil and swab ear gently to clean.

## Nail trimming tips

■ For black nails, use a strong penlight to locate the quick.

■ Try diamond files for nail trimming. They come in a variety of shapes, materials and grits. Start with the finest grit and work up. File in the direction of the nail grain and gently hold the nail to minimize vibration and movement. Pumice stones also work well for nail shortening.

■ As an alternative to trimming the front nails, put sandpaper on the front and back door and teach your dog to scratch it when she wants to go out.

As time goes by, each grooming will become easier and more enjoyable. You and your canine companion's trust in each other will continue to deepen and strengthen. Your dog may never look perfectly groomed, but as Spanish artist Esteban Vicente said, "You must make the effort for through effort comes joy." Your dog will display your efforts for all to see. Your feelings of connection and harmony will flourish and be joyful. You will, together, bask in the "look" of love. ❧

# 29

# Hygiene Habits

*Although every pooch develops its own grooming repertoire, most lick and nibble, shake and scratch, rub and roll.*

To keep our canine pals looking their best, many of us regularly groom them. But no matter how good a job we think we're doing, our pals are oblivious to our efforts and continue with their own grooming routine. Your dog's grooming efforts aren't geared toward improving its looks, however. Scientists suspect that in the wild, dogs groom to increase their chances of survival by keeping their coat clean and free of parasites and bacteria.

# A Dog's Guide to Grooming

### Licking and nibbling

Your dog uses its tongue and teeth to tackle most of its grooming needs. Dogs lick to clean their coat and their anogenital area. Coat licking also seems to comfort dogs. "It's not unusual for a dog to almost go into a reverie when it's licking," observes Dr. Bruce Fogle, a London-based veterinarian. A dog will often "absent mindedly" stop in mid lick—with its tongue on its body—then suddenly remember what it was doing and resume licking.

Dogs nibble themselves with their small front teeth (incisors) to relieve an itch, dislodge a burr, or remove matted hair. Long-haired pooches often nibble at irritating matted hair between their toes.

## Shaking and scratching

Shaking is the simplest grooming technique dogs use, and scratching is one of the most common. Most dog owners have witnessed (or been soaked by) the water-strewing full-body canine shake that dogs commonly delight in after a bath or swim. And scratching is a ubiquitous canine pastime. Many pooches scratch their forequarters with their hind toenails to relieve itchiness.

## Rubbing and rolling

While dogs usually rub to relieve an itch, some "highly evolved" house dogs have another reason for rubbing. "After a dog has finished its food, it will rub its face along the sofa 'due south,' then 'due north,'" notes Dr. Fogle. As mystifying as it may seem, some experts suspect that "sofa rubbing" is simply your pooch's method of wiping its mouth after a meal.

Rolling comes in two varieties: itch-relieving and scent-immersing. A dog will often roll to scratch an area on its back. But dogs also roll in foul-smelling, decomposing material, such as manure or garbage, to cover themselves with the scent. Scientists have come up with various theories to explain the purpose of this type of rolling. The "perfume" may serve to mask a dog's own scent so it can sneak up on prey; or it may be a way of attracting the attention of other dogs; or the odor may simply appeal to dogs.

# Grooming Gone Awry

Since every dog develops characteristic grooming habits, owners need to know what's normal for their pet. Any change can signal a developing problem, and a close inspection is in order.

## Irritant grooming

If you notice your dog grooming a particular spot more often than usual, check for fleas (or other external parasites), a burr, or a mat of hair. If you discover fleas, talk to your veterinarian about the latest flea-control products. Fleas can cause your dog to lick or nibble a particular spot over and over, creating a "hot spot." If you discover a burr or matted hair, carefully remove the irritant and check the animal's skin for damage. If the skin appears irritated but you can't find a cause, the animal could have a bacterial skin infection. Excessively licking one spot can also indicate localized pain (from arthritis, for example). Have your veterinarian examine your pooch to root out the cause of its overzealous grooming.

## Compulsive grooming

After a thorough examination, your veterinarian may conclude that your dog's excessive grooming isn't due to a medical ailment at all but is instead a compulsive behavior. "Dogs with anxious or hyperactive temperaments tend to be predisposed to grooming disorders," explains Dr. Nicholas Dodman, director of the Behavior Clinic at Tufts University School of Veterinary Medicine. For these dogs, a moderate amount of stress (sometimes stemming from boredom or from restrictions on activity) can trigger a grooming compulsion. But—given enough stress—any dog can develop an "excessive grooming habit," with licking the most common manifestation. "A dog will start to lick itself when it's bored or has its goals frustrated," says Dr. Dodman. But licking may become an entrenched habit, occurring even when the dog isn't under stress. Compulsive licking can be so relentless that the animal licks off its hair and damages the underlying skin, creating an ulcerated sore (lick granuloma). Some dogs—particularly small ones—compulsively groom between their toes or chew their toenails excessively.

## Compulsion control

While preventing compulsive disorders is easier than treating them, the techniques for both are the same. You need to eliminate as much stress as possible from your dog's daily life and then—since stress reduction often isn't enough—you'll need to increase its exercise, evaluate its diet, and give it chew toys to keep it busy. Exercise spurs the release of brain chemicals that make a dog feel good and stabilize its mood. A diet lower in energy may help decrease your dog's excitability. And lots of safe chew toys—especially ones you can hide treats inside—will help keep your pet busy when you aren't around. "You want as much of your dog's day occupied with wonderful things as possible," says Dr. Dodman.

Unfortunately, some cases of compulsive grooming are so entrenched that making the above changes won't cure the disorder. In such cases, your veterinarian may prescribe an antiobsessional medication to help your pooch overcome its compulsion. ❧

# 30

# Nailed!

*A little technique and good clippers make
the process bearable for you
and your dog.*

Keeping your dog's nails neatly trimmed is important for healthy feet. It is vitally important to teach your dog to accept nail trimming as part of his regular grooming routine. If you start with a puppy or a young dog, wait until she is resting quietly on the floor after a play session, gently clip off the tip end of one or two nails, feed her tasty treats and tell her what a great dog she is, she will grow up thinking that nail trimming is a wonderful thing.

There are several common mistakes that dog owners make when trimming nails. The first is clipping a nail too short (or "quicking" the dog) which causes pain and bleeding and immediately teaches the dog that nail trimming is not fun. This happened to a young puppy of mine, and it took more than a year of desensitization to convince him to accept his pedicure calmly again.

The second major mistake is trying to trim all the dog's nails in one session. This is fine once the dog learns that nail trimming is a positive thing, but until then, physically restraining a flailing, panicking pooch while insisting that every nail is clipped only makes matters worse. Take the time to do nails one or two at a time, using treats and games to make it fun.

Finally, using poor equipment can make the even most accommodating dog fear nail trimming. Dull blades, tools with only poor visibility (and thus, encourage quicking), and awkward clipper construction can turn nail trimming sessions into nightmares.

But steer clear of the quick—the nail's sensitive interior region that contains nerves and blood vessels. In dogs with light-colored nails, the quick is visibly pink. But even if your dog's nails are dark, you can reduce the risk of painful (and bloody) quick-nicking.

# Some Pointers:

*The goal of nail trimming is to clip enough extra nail to enable the dog to stand and walk comfortably, without clipping the nail so short that you hit the blood vessel. The pink vessel is easy to see in white nails; in black nails you have to clip conservatively, in small increments.*

It's really a safe and simple procedure; one that most dog owners can easily learn to perform on their dogs.

Because young dogs often wear their nails down naturally by running on hard rough surfaces, we tend to overlook the importance of teaching them to accept nail trimming. Then, when the dog ages, slows down, and needs help with those nails, the procedure is seriously traumatic. Shelter workers and veterinarians tell horror stories of elderly dogs unable to walk because their nails have curled around and grown through their pads.

■ Clip frequently. Every time you clip your dog's nails, the quicks recede. Conversely, the quicks of infrequently trimmed nails grow outward.

■ Settle for bits and pieces. Clip off only narrow slices at a time. Stop when you see a black dot (the end of the quick) in the center of the gray-white cut surface.

■ Use sharp trimmers. Consider clippers equipped with guards to prevent you from cutting too close.

■ Prevent squirming. Teach your dog to be a more cooperative "clipee" by handling its feet often and using food treats as rewards during nail-trimming sessions.

# Nail Clippers We Like

To help you with equipment choices, we tested four nail trimmers on four relatively willing subjects who were accustomed to having their nails "done."

*From left: Oster's Electric Nail Grinder, "Vista" dog Nail Clipper (not recommended), "White" Nail Scissors and Resco's guillotine nail clippers.*

■ **White Nail Scissors** (4-1/2" for small animals): These scissors were advertised for use with small to medium breeds, and our Approval rating applies to small dogs only.

These scissors are made of nickel-plated steel. They appear solid and well-made and are affordably priced. They work just like a pair of scissors. But while they clipped an eight-pound Pomeranian's nails easily, they required more force than seemed appropriate to cut through the nails of a 25-pound terrier mix.

The solid construction and simplicity of these scissors was appealing, but their application would be limited to cats and very small dogs.The packaging they came in was disappointing—a plain plastic sleeve with no instructions. If your dog is 15 pounds or less, you could give these a try. For anything larger than a Lhasa, keep reading.

■ **Resco Guillotine Nail Clippers**: These are the old stand-by nail clippers familiar to many owners. The ominous "guillotine" name comes from the fact that the dog's nail is inserted through an opening and the blade slices down to chop it off. Without a "safety stop," the owner must control how much of the nail is inserted through the hole (not an easy task with a wiggling dog). And, as the package instructs, it's important to slice off only a small amount at a time in order to avoid "quicking" the dog.

This has long been a favorite nail-trimming tool. It gives a better view of how much nail is being cut than does the scissors-style clippers. The tool fits solidly in the hand and is easy to grasp and hold. The snug blade fit allows for a clean cut. And, best of all, the blades are replaceable. When you start to find ragged edges on your dog's newly trimmed nails, it's time for a new blade. And, the price is right.

## Top Pick:

■ **Oster Electric Nail Grinder**: This is the tool for the connoisseur of nail trimmers. It is routinely used in the dog-show world to achieve the nub-short nails in vogue for the show ring. It is available in electric and cordless models, and works like a charm, effortlessly grinding away unwanted nail material. Effortlessly, that is, if your dog will allow you anywhere near with the grinder turned on!

Two of our four test dogs tolerated the tool with some initial resistance that was overcome by the liberal use of liver treats. Both dogs were tense about the procedure; it would take additional desensitization to get them as relaxed about this tool as they are with guillotine clippers. The results of the trim were beautiful—short, rounded nails—shorter than if they had been trimmed with the guillotine clippers.

However, our other two test dogs wanted nothing to do with the noisy, vibrating machine. They would stay close for liver bribes when the machine was turned on, but feeling the vibrations against their nails was more than either could tolerate. For these two, a serious desensitization program would have to be implemented before we could successfully grind their nails.

If you are planning to show your dog in the breed ring, the Oster Nail Grinder is a must. Be prepared to spend a considerable amount of time desensitizing your dog to get him or her to accept it. But if you are the average dog owner who just wants to keep your dog's nails in reasonable shape, the Oster Nail Grinder may be more tool than you will ever need.

One last caution: Don't count on the package instructions to help you put the Grinder together.

## Not Recommended:

■ **Vista Dog Nail Clipper** (with Safety Stop): We purchased the medium size clipper, and found it perfectly capable of cutting the nails of our 75-pound Australian cattle dog mix. But, while advertised as having "heavy steel blades," the clipper did not appear as well constructed as the previously described nail scissors—in fact the plastic handles appear downright cheap; it is doubtful if they would stand up to heavy use. The instructions are well-illustrated, clear, easy to understand, and include that all-important warning: "Avoid cutting off too much at one time." The safety stop is an interesting feature, and may inspire confidence in the nervous, first-time owner/clipper, but would just get in the way for a more experienced nail trimmer. (It is removable.)

The biggest complaint: the blades don't line up tightly against each other, so they tend to leave ragged edges on the clipped nail. Skip this one; there are better clippers available at better prices. ❧

# 31

# Lather Up!

*Dog shampoos are different from people shampoos;*
*some have ingredients deleterious*
*to your pooch's health. We help you separate the*
*good from the bad.*

Dogs in the wild don't need baths. Why do our dogs? Well, they don't need baths, but if they want to live in our homes, and sometimes even sleep in our beds, they have to look and smell cleaner than dogs normally do.

Shampoos can be formulated for general cleaning, or for specific purposes, such as killing fleas or soothing irritated skin. Since there are more effective methods of accomplishing both of these tasks, we'll focus only on the sudsy substances that do the best job of cleaning your dog's hair, without irritating his skin, or making him sick.

## Toxic Ingredients?

Yes, there are shampoos that can have deleterious effects on your dog's health. The most toxic ingredients are found in shampoos intended to kill fleas, but a few can be found in ordinary shampoos.

Given the variety and number of products available, we recommend that you avoid products containing any of the ingredients below. Each has been linked to a health hazard, and though they may be present only in tiny amounts, there are safer alternatives available. This list is from *Dr. Pitcairn's Complete Guide to Natural Health for Dogs & Cats*, by Richard Pitcairn, DVM:

- Anise oil
- Boric acid

- Benzene hexacholoride
- Benzethonium chloride
- Chloranil
- DDD
- Depentene
- Dimethyl phthalate
- Menthols
- Napthalene
- Pine tar
- Sodium arsenite
- Sodium cresylate
- Xylene

# Shampoo Selection Criteria

■ Ingredients listed on the container! It seems obvious, but unlike food manufacturers, shampoo makers are not required to list their ingredients on the bottle. But without an ingredients list, a person can't determine the quality of the ingredients nor whether it contains potentially harmful products or chemicals that an individual dog may be allergic to.

■ A shampoo that doesn't harm the dog, us, or the environment. We give extra points to manufacturers who deliver their product in a recyclable container.

■ A reasonable price. The price of a shampoo has more to do with the cost of the maker's advertising than the cost of the materials used in its manufacture.

# Getting into the Tub

Based on our first requirement, we eliminated roughly 70 percent of the dog shampoos on the shelves of our pet stores. Few makers of these products see fit to list their ingredients on the label. Well-known shampoos such as Hartz' Love Your Dog Shampoo, Miracle Corp. of Australia's Miracle Coat Premium Pet Shampoo, Lambert Kay's Groom & Glo, Pet Botanics' Herbal Shampoo, Sergeant's Fur-So-Fresh, and Natural Research People's Nature First Herbal Shampoo, and PurePet's Pure Care are among those guilty.

We brought home a bag full of products that did list the contents, called the neighbors (asking for dog bath "volunteers"), and turned on the hose.

We washed quite a few dogs, but failed to ascertain much of a difference between the coat quality or shine of the dogs that had been scrubbed with different shampoos. In desperation, and much to the consternation of our housemates, we took a half a dozen dog shampoos into our own showers, and tried them on our own hair!

While we found no great differences from one dog shampoo to the next, we did find them to be generally different from our "people" shampoos.

---

LATHER IS FUN. LATHER MAKES YOU FEEL

LIKE YOU'RE ACCOMPLISHING SOMETHING.

---

For one thing, each of the shampoos we tried was noticeably thinner than the shampoos we're accustomed to. Considering that dog baths often take place in less than ideal circumstances—slippery dogs trying to escape, your back screaming in protest at being hunched over, water flying every which way—soap that runs through your fingers too easily is one more annoyance. It also means you invariably end up using twice as much of it to get enough onto your dog.

Each of the shampoos shared another characteristic—they lathered much less than our regular "people" shampoos. We kept in mind that this has nothing to do with their ability to clean, but we still missed the lather. Lather is fun. Lather makes you feel like you're accomplishing something.

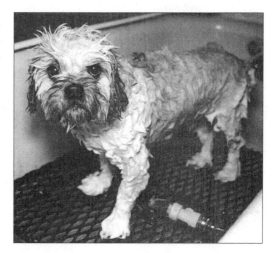

On the other hand, each of them rinsed out quickly and easily.

Musing in the shower, we thought, "These shampoos work so well, why not use them on our hair all the time?" The answer is . . . they cost more than the kind we usually use! So why shouldn't you use "people" shampoo on your dog? If your shampoo works well, is less expensive than your dog's brand, and has none of the potentially harmful ingredients listed above, go ahead!

# Top Dog Shampoos

Keep in mind that there are hundreds of dog shampoos on the market. Shampoos that are better than our picks may exist, and products that are worse than our pans may also. When searching for products to either recommend or review unfavorably, we try to call out examples that are familiar or easily accessible to most shoppers, and that are most representative of the variety of products available. More important than attempting to give you the name of the single most marvelous shampoo in the world, we are trying to teach you how to recognize the hallmarks of good as well as sub-par products.

■ **Dr. Goodpet's Pure Shampoo**: This shampoo was one of the few we found in a recyclable (#2) bottle. It was also one of the few that made our dog washers think the dogs washed with it felt softer and smoother than the dogs washed with the other shampoos. On the other hand, it was one of the most expensive shampoos we tried.

Contains: de-ionized water, coconut oil liquid soap, organic protein, vitamin E, aloe vera, and jojoba oil.

■ **Brookside Soap Inc.'s Best Friend Pet Soap**: The most environmentally friendly shampoo of them all. Best Friend is packaged simply in a 100 percent recycled (and recyclable) paper wrapper that was printed with soy ink. Its label also boasts, "No animal ingredients, never animal tested." Despite our initial concern about the "latherability" of a bar shampoo, it bubbled with the best of them.

Contents: Saponified oils of coconut, palm, and olive, plantain leaf, slippery elm bark, jojoba oil, and essential oils of pennyroyal, citronella, eucalyptus, cedarwood, sage, and tea tree.

■ **8 in 1 Pet Products' Perfect Coat Hypoallergfenic Shampoo**: The most economical of our selections. Contents: water, sodium laureth sulfate, disodium oleamido MEA sulfosuccinate, cocamide DEA, disodium cocoamphodiacetate, cocamidopropyl betaine, sodium chloride, glycerin, aloe vera gel.

■ **Pet Gold's Herbal Hypoallergenic Shampoo**: First, the herbs promised in the "Herbal" title seem to refer to the sole identifiable plant ingredient: aloe vera. However, since aloe appears third on the list of ingredients, it might be present in a high enough quantity to display its skin-soothing qualities.

We're not concerned about the presence of propylene glycol here, though we have warned you about its inclusion in dog foods. First of all, it's not ingested in this venue, and second, it's well down on the list of ingredients.

Contains: water, cocoamidopropyl betaine, aloe vera extract, cocoglutamate TEA, lauramide DEA, propylene glycol, PEG 150 distearate, diazolidinyl urea, methyl paraben, propyl paraben, citric acid.

## Almost Made the List...

■ **Burt's Bees, Inc.'s Oat Straw Pet Soap**: Rules were made to be broken—if there is a good enough reason. We just finished saying that unless a shampoo maker lists the ingredients on the label, you shouldn't buy it. But here's a product with every indication of being a super shampoo—without a complete list of ingredients. The partial list sure looks good, but . . . Dang! Without the complete list, we're at a loss to certify this product as completely safe.

This was the best-smelling and best-lathering shampoo on our list, and its 100 percent recycled cardboard box says it is an all-vegetable product containing oat straw, rosemary, rue, comfrey, citronella, and many more botanical ingredients. It might be worth a call to the company to find out what else is in there.

## Reading the Fine Print

You can learn so much from reading labels, but the manufacturers of cosmetic products (human and canine) are often reluctant to give their consumers too much information, perhaps because most products are more similar than their makers like to admit.

Sometimes the only differences between an expensive shampoo and an inexpensive one are the last few ingredients—which means there is very little difference between them at all.

Contents are required to be listed on the label in descending order of their presence in the product, until you get to the substances that represent less than one percent of the mixture; then they may be listed in any order at all. Since shampoos are usually about 70 to 90 percent water, by the time you get to the preservative or fragrance ingredients (often midway through the list), each substance listed comprises less than one percent of the total content—a minute quantity, and not enough to make an appreciable difference to the effectiveness of the shampoo.

For this reason, we're rather unimpressed with products whose labels proclaim them to be "herbal shampoos," for instance, with herbs appearing last on the ingredients list.

Don't be discouraged if you see long, impossible-to-pronounce chemicals when you look at ingredients lists. While long names are often an indication of unhealthy substances in food products, they are the norm in cosmetic ingredients. In fact, by referring to the list below, which identifies the most common safe ingredients found in shampoo, grouped according to their function, you can easily confirm the purpose and safety of every ingredient in the bottle.

## Cleansing agents
All shampoos contain one or more of these cleansing agents. These help remove dirt and oil from the hair and skin.

Ammonium laureth sulfate; Ammonium lauryl sulfate; Cococamphodiacetate; Cocamidopropyl betaine; Sodium cocoglyceryl ether sulfonate; Sodium laureth sulfate; Sodium lauryl sarcosinate; Sodium lauryl sulfate.

## Lathering Agents
These ingredients are added to shampoos to create lather. Contrary to popular belief, lather does not actually clean the hair. The physical process of building and then rinsing away the lather, however, helps distribute the cleansing agents evenly around the hair. As a rule, people feel better about shampoos that create a lot of lather, but it's strictly a psychological advantage.

Interestingly, the amount of lather you get while shampooing is affected by the amount of oil and debris in the fur. The cleaner the hair, the more lather you will get when using the shampoo. Some shampoo makers instruct their users to shampoo twice; if you do, you'll notice the lather increases on the second round.

Cocamide MEA; Lauramide MEA; Lauric DEA; Polysorbate-20.

## Conditioners
These agents moisturize the hair, make it easy to comb, and smoother to the touch.

Amino acids; Collagen; Panthenol; Protein.

## Humectants
Humectants are agents in shampoos that attract and hold water in the hair, making it feel full, soft, and thick.

Glycerin; Glycols; Glycosphingolipids; Hyaluronic acid; Mucupolysaccharides; Sodium PCA; Sorbitol.

## Quaternary Ammonium Compounds

These ingredients give hair a slick feel.

Behenalkonium betaine; Behentrimonium chloride; Benzalkonium chloride; Cetrimoniummchloride; Dicetydimonium chloride; Quaternium-18; Stearalkonium chloride.

## Thickeners

These ingredients are responsible for the shampoo's thickness:

Caprylic acid; Cetyl alcohol; Glycol stearate; Hydrogenated lanolin; Palmitic acid; PEGs; Stearyl alcohol.

## Preservatives

These agents are crucial to the shampoo because they help keep contamination of the many ingredients to a minimum.

Methylparaben; Phenoxyethanol; Propylparaben; Quaternium 15.

# Bathing Options

*In mild weather, bathing Rover outside with a garden hose is one alternative—if he doesn't mind cold water. But many temperature-sensitive pooches won't tolerate such treatment. And in winter, owners in many parts of the country don't have this option.*

*So what's the owner of a dirty dog to do? You can take advantage of the "dog washes" sponsored by local humane societies or animal shelters and support two good causes at once—your dog's hygiene and the welfare of homeless dogs. But these events don't always coincide with your dog's latest roll in something raunchy.*

*Taking your dog to a groomer can be a convenient alternative, but you still have to spend time finding a reputable groomer with the proper equipment and facilities. Some dogs don't take kindly to handling by strangers, so factor in your dog's temperament when you consider whether to hire a groomer. The advent of mobile dog-grooming vans and pick-up/drop-off services has expanded the options and largely eliminated the logistical hassles, but you usually pay a premium for such convenience.*

*Self-service dog-wash parlors, a growing trend in some*

*parts of the country, have the advantages of equipment specifically designed for bathing dogs and do-it-yourself cost savings. The best of these facilities offer sanitized, ergonomically positioned tubs with humane restraint devices; no-slip flooring; water delivered at a safe pressure and temperature; no-clog drains; grooming tables with dryers; and well-trained staff to help novices get started.*

# The Skinny on "Natural" Skin-Care Products

When faced with the abundance of dog shampoo and skin-care products offered in pet stores and catalogs, many people opt for so-called "natural" products, believing they are inherently better than their synthetic counterparts. But "natural" is not necessarily synonymous with "nontoxic." "There is no product, natural or synthetic, to which some animals won't react adversely," notes Dr. R. L. Robbins, a veterinarian with Clinical Toxicology Resource Associates in Tolono, IL.

Many natural shampoos and skin-care products contain oils distilled from pennyroyal, citrus fruit, and the Australian melaleuca tree. When used as directed, these ingredients may help repel (and even kill) parasitic insects and heal minor skin irritations or infections. But these oils can be absorbed through a dog's skin and, if overused, can cause toxic reactions ranging from severe skin inflammation and excessive salivation to loss of muscle coordination and seizures.

The fact that natural shampoos and skin-care products are not regulated by the U.S. Food and Drug Administration or the Environmental Protection Agency may not mean they're less safe than synthetic products, but it does mean they're not required to be as thoroughly tested. Sometimes, the actual concentrations of active ingredients are not listed on the product labels, and without regulatory oversight, quality control during manufacturing may be compromised. Moreover, if health problems arise with nonregulated natural products, manufacturers are not obligated to inform consumers about these problems.

If your dog shows any sign of an adverse reaction within 2 to 8 hours after bathing or the application of any skin-care product, contact your veterinarian immediately. Better yet, to avoid such a scenario, before you use any "natural" shampoo or skin-care product that's not labeled to your satisfaction, call the manufacturer for a complete list of ingredients and their concentrations. (If the manufacturer doesn't answer your questions satisfactorily, don't use the product.) Then ask your veterinarian if those constituents and amounts are likely to harm your dog.

Also, if any product looks or smells "off," don't use it. If improperly stored, some aromatic oils can degrade into harmful turpentine-like compounds. Finally, whether you use natural or synthetic products, always read the label and follow usage directions. If those directions include rinsing, be sure to rinse your dog thoroughly. ❧

# 32

# Paws & Pads

*Protecting paws and pads is part of
good dog care,
even in warm months.*

A s any Iditarod musher will tell you, a dog is only as fleet as his feet let him be. Sled dogs are certainly among the least pampered working dogs, but you might be surprised to see how much time is lavished on the care of Husky feet. And while most of us don't demand quite as much from our dogs, it makes sense to include good paw care in your regular grooming regimen. For working dogs and dogs who accompany owners on hikes and other outings over rough terrain, a good bootie can keep the paws and pads from getting injured or protect an already injured paw and keep everyone on the move.

## Anatomy of the Foot

To understand how to take care of a dog's feet, you need to understand how they work. It may not be obvious at first glance, but your dog walks on his toes. If you imagine a dog's back leg as a human leg, you notice that a dog's "heel," called a hock, is only on the ground when a dog is sitting. On the front leg, the dog has a recognizable elbow leading to the wrist, which does not touch the ground when a dog moves. The dog rests not on his "palms," as a human on all fours would, but on his front toes.

Other animals, such as the horse, share this unusual anatomy, but the dog's paw, with its pads and nails, provides traction and shock absorption. Healthy pads are rough and tough; thick enough to avoid tearing on sharp surfaces and rough enough to prevent slipping on smooth surfaces. Very active dogs have naturally tough feet from frequent exercise, but even the toughest pads can be sliced open by a piece of broken glass or jagged rock. And dogs whose main exercise comes from walks on sidewalks may be prone to dry or cracked pads from the sand and salt used during the winter months.

While all dogs' paws are anatomically similar, the huge variety of dog breeds means there are some key differences in the shape of the foot. Many working breeds have standards which call for compact or "cat feet." Breeds with "cat feet" include the Akita, Doberman Pinscher, Giant Schnauzer, Newfoundland, and Old English Sheepdog. Dogs with "hare feet" have two center toes which are longer than the side toes. Many toy breeds have hare feet, such as the Bedlington and Skye Terriers. Sight hounds, such as the Borzoi and the Greyhound, also have hare feet. Finally, some breeds that work in water are bred for webbed feet. The Newfoundland, Chesapeake Bay Retriever, Portugese Water Dog, and German Wirehaired Pointer all have webbing between their toes.

# Paw Grooming

Dog owners can do a lot to prevent injuries and protect their dogs' feet. First, include the paws in your regular grooming regimen. Keep

 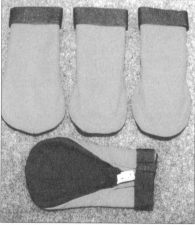

*Left: Walkabout Boots; Right: Wolf Pack Summer Pad Protectors.*

the fur trimmed between a dog's toes and pads so that ice balls don't have a chance to collect when your dog is playing in the snow—or nettles and burrs in the fields and woods. Make sure your dog's nails are trimmed to the proper length—not quite touching the ground when standing comfortably. Always rinse your dog's paws with warm water after walking on salty or sandy sidewalks. It's also a good idea to check your dog's paws after hiking in the woods for burrs, twigs, or caked mud.

Chronically wet feet can lead to secondary yeast infection, which leads to increased licking and inflammation. After rinsing off your dog's feet, towel them dry. If you find that salt or other de-icer you use on your walks and drive hurts your dog, try Safe Paw. It's salt-free and nontoxic and won't burn or injure a dog's paws. It's much more expensive than a regular salt-based ice melter, but can solve a problem if you don't want to use booties.

If the pads seem dry or brittle, try coating them with a little petroleum jelly or Bag Balm after going outside. Pad conditioners, such as Tuf-Foot, go one step further by actually toughening the pads. It's not cheap, but it's worth it if it prevents injury especially if you spend a lot of time outdoors with your dog. You should only use these products if the pads are soft and injured. Otherwise, let nature take its course.

And of course, keep your dog's toenails clipped, as we've outlined inan earlier chapter.

## Consider Booties

Another option for dogs who rough it on snow or rocky trails, who have had paw or pad injuries, or who spend many hours walking over hot or icy surfaces are dog booties. While they might seem extravagant or impractical at first glance, booties can help prevent injuries from sharp rocks and broken glass, and are a boon to those who cross-country ski, hunt or hike regularly with their dogs. You can keep your dog from trying to pull them off by putting them on right before your hike or run. Most dogs are too caught up in their exercise to stop and fuss with well-fitting booties. Be careful with sudden turns and stops: the enclosed claws and pads won't brake or react as sharply as they do when exposed.

There are a handful of different brands available. Most make a winter bootie and a summer bootie because of the different demands made on the paws by snow and ice and by hot, hard pavement and rough rock. You'll of course want a set of four. Wolf Packs LLC makes nylon-

and-Velcro dog booties for summer use and Polartec-and-Velcro booties for winter use. They come in four different sizes, are well-made and thoughtfully constructed. However, the smallest size is designed for a dog with a two-and-a-half-inch pad, not including claws. That's typically a 40- to 50-pound dog. Smaller dogs are out of luck.

The Comfort-Fit Dog Boots come in a small size that will fit even toy breeds, five-20 lbs. They're inexpensive, but larger breeds may wear them out quickly. The Walkabout Boots are expensive and, since they're made of neoprene, really suitable only for snow or very wet conditions. We'd choose the Wolf-Packs for larger dogs and the Comfort-Fit for smaller dogs.

## When Injuries Occur

*Sometimes, despite the best paw care, injuries do occur. Split toenails are always painful and merit a trip to the vet to assess how bad the damage is. Sometimes anesthesia is necessary to remove the remaining nail. On the other hand, pad injuries, even when pieces of the pad are missing, will usually heal by themselves. Applying antibiotic ointment can help prevent infection, and the pad will be back to normal within two weeks. If there is swelling or unusual heat in the pad, however, consult your veterinarian, in case an infection or abscess is brewing. And if your dog seems to have chronic foot pain, it could be a sign of a more serious medical condition, such as phemphigus, lupus, or Lyme disease. Your vet can help determine if any of these conditions are present.* ❧

# Appendix

## Raw Foods, Supplies & Supplements

Florazyme (made by Pet's Friend, 800-868-1009) or ProZyme; (800-522-5537)

Nutrition Coalition, Fargo, ND Ph: (800) 447-4793/218-236-9783; F: (218) 236-6753 www.willardswater.com' Willard Water concentrate

Steve's Real Food for Dogs, Eugene, Or Ph: (541) 683-9950; F: (541) 683-2035; Frozen and freeze-dried raw meat dog food

Fresh Food Momma, Fair Oaks, CA Ph: 916- 967-6255; Frozen raw meat diets for dogs

Pat McKay, Inc., Pasadena, CA Ph: (800) 975-7555/ 626-296-1120; F: (626) 296-1126 www.home1.gte.net/patmckay; Frozen raw foods, supplements, nutritional consultations

Natural Lifestyle Supplies, Asheville NC Ph (800) 752-2775 or (828) 254-9606; Organic seeds, grains, Japanese salad presses

No Bones About It Pet Care, North Haledon, NJ Ph (973) 595-1451; Raw meat diets, Stand. Proc. supplments.

NutriBiotic, Lakeport, CA. 2 oz. bottle @ $10 (800) 225-4345; Grapefruit Seed Extract Liquid Concentrate

Sullivan Creek Distributors, Cascade, MT. ; Ph: (888) 406-4066/(406) 468-2144; 35% Food Grade Hydrogen Peroxide; 1 pt. bottle @ $11

Wysong Institute, Midland MI Ph: (517) 631-0009; F: (517) 631-8801;wysong@tm.net; Natural supplements

Celeste Yarnall, Beverly Hills, CA Ph: (888) 235-7387/(310) 278-1385 Raw meat diets, supplements, nutritional consultations

Pat McKay, Inc, Animal Nutrition, Pasadena, CA  Ph: (800) 975-7555, or (626) 296-1120

Animal Food Services, Inc., Iola, WI (800) 743-0322

Russell Swift, DVM, Tamarac, FL (561) 391-5615; Veterinary Nutrition Consultant; Raw food diets, custom diets and diet supplements.

## Public Resources

Meat Safety Questions: United State Department of Agriculture, Food Safety Department; (800) 535-4555;

expert answers to consumer questions. 10 a.m. to 4 p.m., EST

The Humane Society of the United States Flyer #PM2098) spells out the dangers of leaving a dog inside a parked car. The flyers are sold in packets of 100. Upon request, the Humane Society will send out packets for $3.50 each, plus $3 shipping and handling. Make checks payable to: The Humane Society of the United States, 2100 L St., NW, Washington, DC 20037. Residents of CA, CT, DC, FL, IL, MA, MD, NJ, OH, TX, VT, and NY add appropriate sales tax

# Food

## Premium
**California Natural**: Natura Pet Products; PO Box 271, Santa Clara, CA 95052; (800) 532-7261 or (408) 261-0770(800) 532-7261.

**Flint River**: Flint River Ranch 1243 Columbia Avenue, Riverside, CA 92507; (909) 682-5048(408) 464-1178.

**Petguard Lifespan**: PetGuard PO Box 728, Orange Park, FL 32067 (800) 874-3221/(800) 331-7527 in FL /904) 264-8500 or; (800) 874-3221.

## Top 10 dry
Back to Basics (Chicken formula) Beowulf Natural Feeds, Inc. PO Box 151, Altmar, NY 13302 (800) 219-2558 /(315) 298-7366

**California Natural**
See Above

**Canidae**
Canidae Corporation
PO Box 3610, San Luis Obispo, CA 93403; (800) 398-1600 or (805) 544-4470

**Flint River**
See Above

**Innova**
Natura Pet Products
PO Box 271, Santa Clara, CA 95052 (800) 532-7261 or (408) 261-0770

**Limited Diet**
Innovative Veterinary Diets (division of Nature's Recipe)
341 Bonnie Circle, Corona, CA 91720
(800) 359-4483 or (909) 278-4280

**PetGuard LifeSpan**
See Above

**Pinnacle**
Breeder's Choice
16321 E. Arrow Highway, Irwindale, CA 91706
(800) 255-4286/(626) 334-9301

**Solid Gold**
1483 N. Cuyamaca, El Cajon, CA 92020; West Coast (800) DOG-HUND;East Coast (800) 521-0010; (619)258-1914

**Wysong Maintenance**
Wysong Corporation
1880 North Eastman, Midland, MI 48640; (800) 748-0233/(517) 631-0009

## Top 10 canned

**Breeder's Choice Avo-Derm**: (800) 255-4286.
**Solid Gold**: (800) DOG-HUND.
**Hi-Tor Eno Diet**: (800) 331-5144.
**California Natural**: (800) 532-7261
**Canidae**: (800) 398-1600.
**Innova**: (800) 532-7261.
**Wysong Maintenance**: (517) 631-0009.
**Neura 95** (95% Beef): (800) 225-0904.
**Petguard** (with Coleman Beef): 800) 874-3221.
**Spot's Stew**: (800) 426-4256.

## Top treats

**California Natural Health Bar**
Natura Pet Products, Santa Clara, CA; (800) 532-7261

**Doggie Divines** (Chicken Carrot)
Brunzi's Best, Garrison, NY; Ph: (877) 278-6947

**Liver Biscotti**
Woolf Products, Concord, CA; Ph: (888) 500-3647

**Liver Crisps**
Dancing Dog Bakery, Creswell, OR; Ph: (541) 895-5950

**Burt's Bones**
Burt's Bees, Inc., Raleigh, NC; Ph: (800) 849-7112

**Howlin' Gourmet** (Peanutty & Honey); Dancing Paws Bakery, Pacific Palisades, CA; Ph: (888) 644-7297

**Mr. Barky's Vegetarian Dog Biscuits**
PetGuard, Orange Park, FL; Ph: (800) 874-3221

**Poochie Pretzels**
Molly's Gourmutt Bakery, Poway, CA; Ph: (887) 468-6888

## Household products

Green Seal products, call (202) 331-7223.

## Books

Complete Guide to Natural Health for Dogs & Cats; 1995, Richard Pitcairn, DVM & Susan Hubble Pitcairn ISBN 0-87596-243-2; Raw foods for animals; nutrition, recipes.

The Encyclopedia of Natural Pet Care; 1998, CJ Puotinen ISBN 0-87983-797-7; Natural diets and supplements.

Give Your Dog A Bone 1993, Dr. Ian Billinghurst ISBN 0-646-16028-1; Diets mainly comprised of "bones and raw food."

It's For The Animals:
A Guided Tour of Natural Care and Resource Directory
1998, Helen L. McKinnon; Ph: (908) 537-4144; Nutrition and veterinary experts; product sources.

The Natural Dog 1994, Mary L. Brennan, DVM ISBN 0-452-27019-7; Healthy diet.

Natural Dog Care
1998, Celeste Yarnall
ISBN 1-885203-47-0
Nutrition, diet suggestions.

Reigning Cats and Dogs
1996, Pat McKay
ISBN 0-9632394-1-4; Raw foods.

The Ultimate Diet
1998, Kymythy R. Schultze
ISBN 0-9664749-1-0
Natural diet; prey animals as role
models for menu

The Complete Herbal Handbook for
the Dog and Cat
Juliette de Bairacli Levy; London,
Faber and Faber, 1953,
rev 1991. ISBN 0-571-16115-4

Feed Your Pup with Bones
Ian Billinghurst, Lithgow, N.S.W.
Australia, 1998.
ISBN 0-958-5925-00

Natural Remedies for Dogs and Cats
CJ Puotinen, Los Angeles,
Keats/NTC Publications, 10/99.

Natural Rearing Directory
P.O. Box 1436, Jacksonville, OR
97530.; Ph: (541) 899-2080, F: (541)
899-3414; ambrican@cdsnet.net;
www.naturalrearing.com.
Annual directory of breeders who
feed raw foods.

The Healing Touch (Newmarket
Press; $10.95); Dr. Michael Fox.
For laypersons interested in general, diagnostic, and therapeutic dog
massage.

## Vitamins/Supplements

Maximum Protection Vitamins &
Minerals: (Dr. Goodpet Laboratories,
8 oz. for about $2.50; 800-222-9932.)

Canine Digestive Enzymes; (Dr.
Goodpet Laboratories, 7 oz.
bottle, about $15; 800-222-9932)

Lipiderm: (Bioglan Animal Products; 60 capsules, about $8; 800-454-
0040)

Prozyme: (Prozyme Products, Inc.;
200 gm bottle, about $17;
(800)-522-5537)

Super Blue Green Algae (SBGA):
Cell Tech, Klamath Falls, OR

Club Vitamin's Pure Sodium Ascorbate Powder: $7.49 for 227 grams
(3.3 cents per gram).Ph: (604) 602-
7284 or www.; club-vitamin.com.

Wholesale Nutrition's Pure Sodium
Ascorbate Powder
$18 for 511 grams (3.5 cents per
gram); (800) 325-2664 or
www.nutri.com.

Orthomolecular Specialties' Mega C
Plus: (408) 227-9334 or
www.belfield.com.

## Skin Care

Oatmeal Soap: Earthbath, 415-771-
1166. For itchy or broken skin. To
make your own oatmeal rinse: Whiz
one cup of dry oatmeal in a blender

and then soak it in two quarts of water for ten minutes. Strain and add half a cup of aloe vera. For fleas, add a teaspoon of citrus oil.

Miracle Groom: available in pet stores, or call 800-575-3515
Dr. Goodpet's Pure Shampoo: $6 /8oz. (800) 222-9932.
Brookside Soap Inc.'s Best Friend Pet Soap: $4.39/4oz. (425) 742-2265.

Perfect Coat Hypoallergenic Shampoo: $7 for 16 oz.; (516) 232-1200.

Pet Gold's Herbal Hypoallergenic Shampoo: $6/12 oz; ; (619) 453-8373.

Burt's Bees, Inc.'s Oat Straw Pet Soap: $6/3.5 oz..(919) 510-8720. ❧

# Index